DISCOVERIN

ROMAN
BRITAIN

DISCOVERING
ROMAN BRITAIN

ANDREW McCLOY AND
ANDREW MIDGLEY

NEW HOLLAND

This edition published in 2008 by New Holland Publishers (UK) Ltd
First published in 2006 by New Holland Publishers (UK) Ltd
London • Cape Town • Sydney • Auckland

www.newhollandpublishers.com

Garfield House, 86–88 Edgware Road, London W2 2EA, United Kingdom

80 McKenzie Street, Cape Town 8001, South Africa

Unit 1, 66 Gibbes Street, Chatswood, NSW 2067, Australia

218 Lake Road, Northcote, Auckland, New Zealand

10 9 8 7 6 5 4 3 2 1

ISBN 978 1 84773 127 2

Publishing Manager: Jo Hemmings
Senior Editor: Kate Michell
Assistant Editor: Kate Parker
Cover Design and Design: Alan Marshall
Cartography: Bill Smuts
Indexer: Dorothy Frame
Production: Joan Woodroffe

Reproduction by Pica Digital Pte Ltd, Singapore
Printed and bound in Singapore by Kyodo Printing Co. Pte Ltd

Photographs appearing on the cover and prelim pages are as follows:
Front cover: Mosaics at Bignor.
Back cover (left to right): Walk around Chester, Hadrian's Wall.

Page 1: Medusa mosaic in bath house at Bignor.
Pages 2–3: Steel Rigg, Hadrian's Wall, Northumberland.
Opposite: Lullingstone Roman Villa, Kent.
Page 6 (top to bottom): The tombstone of cavalry officer Longinus which was
smashed in the Boudican Revolt against Rome, Colchester Museum; Roman bust from
Lullingstone Roman Villa; selection of amphorae at Colchester Museum.
Page 7: Remains of the Roman theatre in St Albans, Hertfordshire.

Stairs to
the Baths

Kitchen
or Store

**South
Wing Room**
Probably a living room

CONTENTS

INTRODUCTION

We find the Romans endlessly fascinating. They may have occupied Britain for only four centuries, and treated the province as something of a political football, but nevertheless, compared to what went before and what came after, there's something of the sophisticated and modern about them that we can relate to. They introduced well-made roads, central heating, grid-plan streets, stylish interior décor, herb racks and even the three-course meal – as well as knocking up Hadrian's Wall in just a few years without a JCB in sight. Although their troops were ruthless and well trained, and flexed their imperial muscle early on, most of the natives (in England, at least) soon began to co-exist with their new Roman masters. The voracious legionary fortresses needed never-ending supplies, while farming estates (villas) produced the food and other goods that were sold and traded in civilian towns like Cirencester and Silchester.

All too soon, however, the Mediterranean visitors departed as their empire began to crumble and the north-western frontier was abandoned. The Romans gave way to new invaders and a new historical phase, but although their temples were smashed and their forts overrun, their *modus operandi* – to use an appropriately Latin term – is still comprehensible to us today. Except that we don't feed our slaves to the lions, of course.

BELOW: Roman tombstones at the Grosvenor Museum in Chester.

As far as the walks themselves are concerned, they are deliberately varied in terms of location, complexion and length in order to reflect the different aspects of life in everyday Roman Britain. A peaceful wander across the handsome wooded slopes surrounding the once sumptuous villas at Bignor (South Downs) and Chedworth (Cotswolds) contrasts with a hill walk through the imposing Brecon Beacons exploring the Roman military road of Sarn Helen. Similarly, you can step out across the Cheviots' wild and invigorating slopes on Dere Street, where the Roman troops marched from England into Scotland, or visit the spectacularly sited Hardknott Fort, high on the Lake District's open fells. There's an easy ramble around Caerleon's river-valley setting in south Wales, where the legionaries went about day-to-day barrack life, but different again is a stroll through urban Chester and York, exploring the historic city walls and charting the evolution of these two important Roman military centres. Everyday life in civilian towns features in the St Albans and Colchester walks, but the pace quickens for a march across north Norfolk's flat countryside on the dead-straight Peddar's Way. Elsewhere, it's patrol duty as we tackle the coast-to-coast barriers of Hadrian's Wall and its lesser-known Scottish counterpart, the Antonine Wall.

There are opportunities to shorten (and lengthen) the overall distance of a few routes, and since several are genuine hill walks, make sure you are properly equipped. Finally, bear in mind that the time given for each outing is only an estimate of the actual walking route – even the easy urban walks will take you far longer once you begin visiting museums and Roman remains along the way. Indeed, given that their occupation was the best part of 2,000 years ago there is still much to see and marvel at, and an exploration of Roman York or Chester is easily a day's outing in itself. The Romans might not have stayed particularly long, but their legacy lives on.

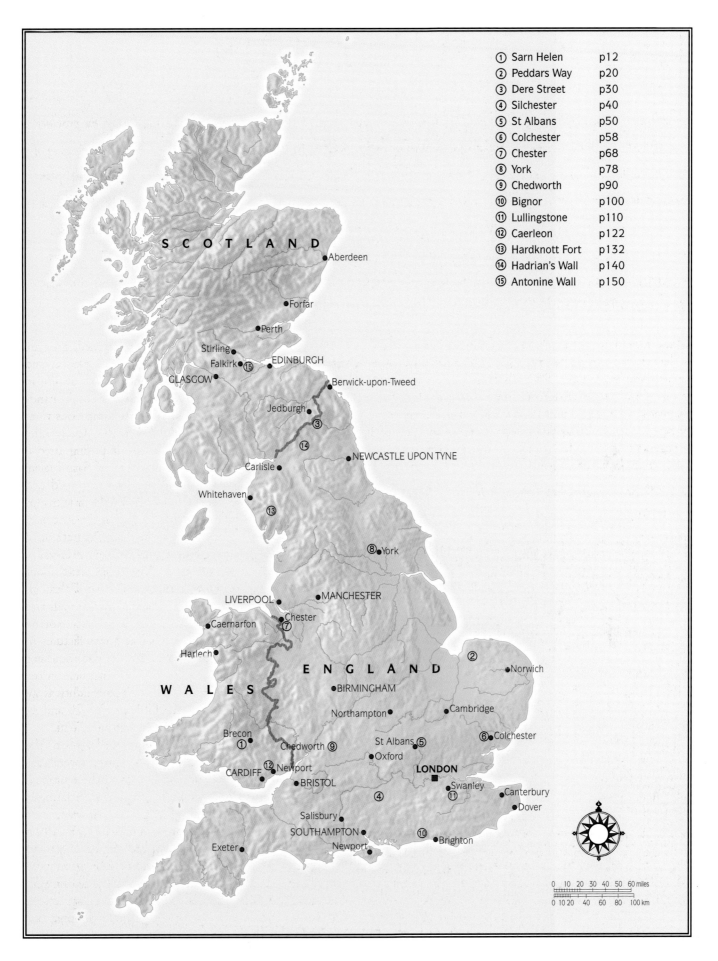

SCOTLAND

Aberdeen

Forfar

Perth

Stirling
Falkirk ⑮   EDINBURGH
GLASGOW   Berwick-upon-Tweed

Jedburgh
③
⑭   NEWCASTLE UPON TYNE
Carlisle

Whitehaven
⑬

⑧ York

LIVERPOOL   MANCHESTER

Caernarfon   Chester
⑦
Harlech

ENGLAND   ②
                            Norwich
WALES   BIRMINGHAM

Northampton   Cambridge

Brecon   St Albans ⑤   ⑥ Colchester
①   Chedworth ⑨   Oxford
CARDIFF ⑫ Newport   LONDON
       BRISTOL   Swanley
④   Canterbury
Salisbury ⑪   Dover
SOUTHAMPTON
Newport   ⑩ Brighton
Exeter

0 10 20 30 40 50 60 miles
0 10 20 40 60 80 100 km

ROMAN ROADS

To the Romans it was simply logical to link towns and garrisons by a network of direct and reliable highways. Troops and supplies could be moved around at speed, and the sight of a detachment of mean-looking legionaries on the march would no doubt cause restless natives a sleepless night. However, the skill of the Roman road-builders was really twofold: the roads themselves were made to a high standard, extremely hard-wearing and frequently raised on a well-drained bed of layered material. But they were also expertly surveyed and their alignment adapted to suit the local terrain – famously straight and no-nonsense in many instances, but elsewhere skilfully negotiating the contours and natural features. The Romans created, in effect, the first road atlas to Britain, and it remains a masterpiece.

OPPOSITE: Roadside memorial – an inscribed stone sits beside the Roman route of Sarn Helen, south of Brecon.

SARN HELEN

THE SECLUDED BEACONS

The lonely upland route from Neath (Nidum) to Brecon, subsequently known as Sarn Helen, remains one of the most evocative of the Roman roads you can still follow on foot today, not so much for the visible remains of forts or Roman buildings but for the sense of isolation and wildness. As you progress through the remote hills and bare moorland on a route so irresistibly direct that it just has to be Roman, you get a sense of what it must have been like for the wary troops. Is that someone at the top of the slope ahead? Are we about to run into an ambush by the Silures? Compared to other Roman roads, Sarn Helen was a relatively minor route, but it was one of a number that converged on the Roman fort at Brecon near the start of this walk and formed part of the Romans' strategic attempt to subjugate Wales. With inhospitable terrain and even more unfriendly natives, Wales was probably not a popular posting among Roman soldiers.

This walk forms a rough figure of eight, based on the Brecon Beacons National Park Mountain Centre, and as such offers several choices. The first loop is an easy walk around the gentle but lofty common of Mynydd Illtud, taking in Iron Age as well as Roman history, and enjoying a superb upland panorama across to the central Beacons.

The second part of the walk is more ambitious but not particularly difficult in clear conditions, and from the Roman road of Sarn Helen it ascends the shapely summit of Fan Frynych. Most of the mountain is a National Nature Reserve, as well as providing a wonderful viewpoint over the surrounding countryside.

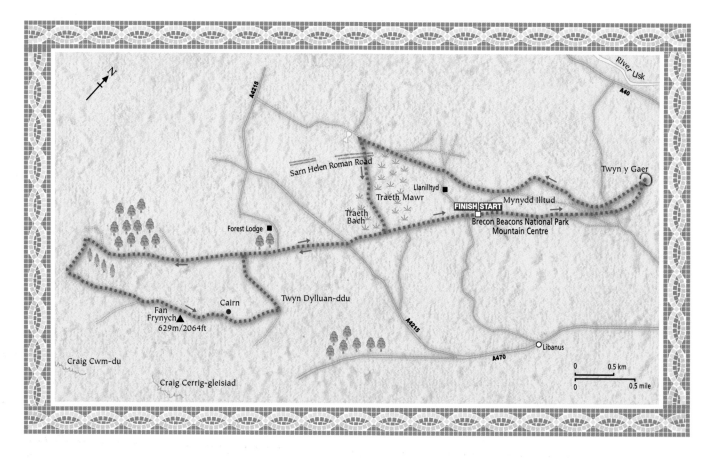

However, at 2,064 feet (629m) high, Fan Frynych is a serious mountain, and it is important that you are suitably equipped and can navigate competently in adverse conditions. If you're reasonably fit and the weather is amenable the whole route provides an invigorating day out, with the prospect of a pot of tea and a tasty slice of bara brith at the Mountain Centre's tearoom at the end. The Roman legionaries were never so pampered!

ABOVE: The hill fort at Twyn y Gaer commands extensive views over the Usk Valley.

Vantage Point across the Usk

The Mountain Centre above Libanus, south-west of Brecon, is the main visitor centre for

SARN HELEN, POWYS

Start & finish: Brecon Beacons National Park Mountain Centre, Libanus, Brecon, GR 977263

Distance: 12 miles/19km

Time: 6 hours

Terrain: A variety of moorland and hill tracks, some of them rough and potentially slippery

Map: OS Outdoor Leisure 12: Brecon Beacons Western & Central areas

Guidebook: *What to see from the Mountain Centre on Foot* — booklet guide from the Mountain Centre

Public transport: *Discover the Brecon Beacons National Park by public transport* — free booklet from local information centres

Information: Mountain Centre 01874 623366; www.breconbeacons.org; Brecon Tourist Information Centre 01874 622485

ABOVE: The Brecon Beacons, viewed from Mynydd Illtud, provide a spectacular mountain backdrop to the walk.

the Brecon Beacons National Park and is open all year round. There are interesting displays and exhibitions about the area, including local history and wildlife, and a well-stocked information centre.

Go out of the main entrance and turn right, then follow the popular grassy track north-eastwards along the common between the clumps of gorse and bracken. There are plenty of minor paths that criss-cross the narrow strip of common, plus two unfenced lanes you cross along the way, but if you are in any doubt simply head up towards the prominent low summit of Twyn y Gaer at the common's northern tip.

The ditch and rampart of this Iron Age hillfort are clear for all to see, with its original entrance facing east. The various banks and mounds on its adjoining slopes are the remains of man-made rabbit warrens, built during the Middle Ages when rabbits were farmed for their meat and fur. The hillfort was well sited, since the modest summit affords commanding views in virtually every direction, and in particular across the Usk valley immediately below. It must surely have been used by the Romans for a lookout position, although the military road they constructed, today known as Sarn Helen and which forms the basis of this walk, probably dropped down to cross the river a little to the north or west. On the far bank, a little over a mile away, the Romans established the fort of Y Gaer (Brecon Gaer).

Looking back towards the Mountain Centre, the main thrust of the Brecon Beacons rises spectacularly to the south-east, with the peaks and ridges radiating out from the

THE ATTEMPT TO CONQUER WALES

The Roman fort near Brecon and the military road which you will be exploring on this walk were constructed as part of the Romans' campaign to subjugate the Celts, but the conquest of Wales was no easy task. South Wales was the home of the Silures tribe, described by Tacitus as swarthy, ferocious, curly-haired warmongers; while among the more inaccessible mountains of mid-Wales lay the Ordovices, whose penchant for battle was legendary. It was clear that the Romans were not welcome in Wales, which posed a problem. On the one hand the Romans wanted to stamp out any sign of rebellion that would threaten their northern empire, but on the other they sought to exploit the natural resources that Wales could offer, especially its minerals. Both the Welsh tribes waged effective guerrilla

campaigns. The Silures were led by Caratacus, a fugitive native leader bitterly opposed to the Romans, and although he was captured, the tribe was not entirely subdued until AD 74 when governor Julius Frontinus decided to station the 2nd Augusta Legion at the new legionary fort of *Isca* or Caerleon (see pages 122–131). Although the Silures were to some extent susceptible to the carrot-and-stick approach, the bloodthirsty Ordovices were ultimately suppressed by brute force four years later, when Frontinus's successor, Agricola, beat them into submission and established forts such as Caernarvon (*Segontium*) in the Conway valley. The Romans were never able to introduce effective civilian rule in Wales, and instead resorted to policing it via a network of military roads, forts and marching camps.

mighty Pen y Fan, which at 2,906 feet (886m) is the highest point in south Wales. Further east are the Black Mountains, above Talgarth and Hay-on-Wye, which mustn't be confused with the Black Mountain (singular), which lies over to the west. In between the Black Mountain and the Beacons is a middle range called Fforest Fawr, and it is on the edge of this (roughly south-west) that the attractive, angular shape of Fan Frynych forms the destination for the second half of the walk.

Leave Twyn y Gaer for a broad, grassy track south-south-westwards through the bracken, which is routinely cut in the autumn and early winter for use as bedding for farm animals under an ancient right known as 'estover'. You will be aiming for the right-hand edge of the common as you walk, the opposite side from the Mountain Centre, and after crossing the road turn right on a well-walked track alongside the perimeter fence. Apart from a small area where the fence (topping a low wall) swings away to the right – here simply go straight on – keep the boundary of the common on the right and continue more or less parallel with the unfenced road on your left. Before long you are walking beside the pleasant, open lane across the common. Ignore the turning on the left for Llanilltyd, and instead continue like this for over a mile as the boggy expanse of Traeth Mawr, a nature reserve and home to snipe and curlew, opens up on your left. Beyond, on the far edge of the common, is a similar marshy section called Traeth Bach. Incidentally, St Illtud (or Illtyd) was an early Welsh saint who lived around the

ABOVE: *Standing stones, such as Maen Llia near the Roman Road east of Fan Nedd, may date back to the Bronze Age.*

5th to 6th century and helped establish Christianity in Wales. He is celebrated at a number of locations in the region, and his body is thought to lie at Llantwit Major, near Bridgend, where he established a monastery.

Towards the end of the common you approach a pond by the roadside. Turn left before the water on a popular track across the middle of the common, which at this point has the feel of moorland. After a couple of hundred metres, the track is crossed by the Roman Road, Sarn Helen, and you can just make out the artificially raised bed of the agger. This foundation of hard gravel or such like was not necessary for much of Sarn Helen, for like many of the upland Roman routes the skilled Roman engineers laid the road directly on to the hard rocky surface.

As if to emphasize the common's historical pedigree, not content with a Roman road and Iron Age hillfort there are also a couple of standing stones to be found on Mynydd Illtud, including one away to your right on the far edge of the common. They are believed to be Bronze Age, and may denote a specific route or boundary, or even have some link with the solstice.

When you reach the far side of the common, and the main route along the eastern perimeter, either turn left for the Mountain Centre (just a few minutes' walk away) or to continue the second part of the walk head right towards Fan Frynych.

A March Up the Mountain

The broad track soon emerges at a road junction, where you should go straight over for the short lane opposite. Where this ends, at Forest Lodge, continue along the wide and scenic track via a couple of gates and out across the north-western foot of Fan Frynych. This, as a noticeboard will testify, is part of the Craig Cerrig-gleisiad National Nature Reserve, which encompasses the whole mountain. It's especially noteworthy for its plant life, with over 500 different types found across the reserve, and given its height and rocky

nature (with inhospitable crags and screes) arctic-alpine varieties such as saxifrages do particularly well here.

Although the track before you is evidently purposeful and well-made, the actual Roman road ran just to the north and doesn't meet up until a little further along, and this route instead was used by traders and drovers taking their goods and animals from south and west Wales to market at Brecon.

After you pass a large conifer plantation on your right the main route swings right, and here take the inviting track straight ahead past a gate that gently climbs the slope (look out for the fir trees directly ahead). It's a gradual, easy route, and as it bears left beyond the firs and climbs higher, you can clearly make out where the Roman road continues across the open moors in a south-westerly direction (there's more on exploring the route further at the end).

Towards the top of the slope the route bends abruptly left – it's where the hitherto wide and sunken track seems to vanish (if you begin to head downhill into the narrow valley of Craig Cwm-du you've gone too far). Now you're on the bare and relatively flat moorland summit: follow the path past the cairn and on to the trig point. Fan Frynych may seem modest in comparison to some of its loftier neighbours, but at 2,064 feet (629m) it's an appreciable height, and with the huge crags of Craig Cerrig-gleisiad on its eastern face it's a mountain that deserves respect.

Standing by the trig point with your back to where you've just come, go straight on (north-east) on a clear grassy track – not the wider and more inviting one to the right. This soon joins a broad, semi-surfaced track that comes in from the right (which has skirted the top of the crags) and begins to descend the broad, main ridge past a cairn. Go through a gate and stile and head downhill, with superb views of Mynydd Illtud and the hillfort at the far end. Approaching Twyn Dylluan-ddu the route reaches a cross-fence, and despite the stile ahead you should turn sharply left on the main track beside the fence, which then drops diagonally down the hillside.

ABOVE: Fan Frynych, viewed from the north-west – the whole mountain is a designated National Nature Reserve.

ABOVE: The tall pillar of Maen Madoc supposedly commemorates Dervacus, son of Justus.

BELOW: The Maiden's Stone, found near Brecon, shows a husband and wife embracing.

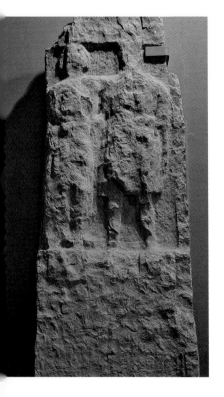

At the bottom turn right to rejoin the approach route from earlier, passing Forest Lodge and crossing back over the road for the open track along the edge of the common to the Mountain Centre.

Exploring Sarn Helen

If the walk has whetted your appetite and you would like to discover more about this most evocative of Roman mountain roads, then get a detailed Ordnance Survey map and plan a further excursion. The route from Neath to Brecon is one of several in Wales that are known, rather confusingly, as Sarn Helen. It was never originally called this, and appears to have gained its name from the Welsh word 'sarn' meaning causeway, together with the name of the 4th-century wife of Emperor Magnus Maximus. According to the Welsh epic *Mabinogion* ('The Dream of Maxen Wledig'), Maximus weds the daughter of a Welsh chieftain called Helen (Elen Lyddawc) and makes her a gift of three Welsh fortresses connected by roads. Another school of thought suggests that 'Helen' is a corruption of 'Lleng', the Welsh for legion, making the route 'the legion's causeway'.

From the western slopes of Fan Frynych you will have already seen the Roman road travelling south-westwards across the high moorland and around the broad shoulder of Fan Nedd. Near the standing stone of Maen Llia it joins the modern road that has zigzagged up from the Senni valley, and the two combine for about a mile until Sarn Helen leaves on a signposted forest track. This is a good stretch to explore, even for just a short outing, for although there is no longer any evidence of the Romans' marching camp among the conifers you can clearly see where the wide, straight track was pitched and its surface expertly laid out. At the far side of the trees the track emerges high above wild and open hillside, with glorious views over an undulating and part-forested landscape seemingly devoid of any human habitation. It's the preserve of meadow pipits and soaring buzzards, and apart from the modern plantations probably little different to the time when Fforest Fawr (the Great Forest) was maintained as a vast royal hunting park before the sheep flocks were introduced in the 19th century.

By the side of the track is a standing stone called Maen Madoc. On the edge of the giant pillar is a Latin inscription, all but illegible, which I'm told reads: 'Dervacus son of Justus. He lies here.' It's claimed that the pillar dates from the 5th or 6th century and the Kingdom of Brycheiniog. Investigations in 1940 revealed that the stone had been re-erected after falling down some time before, and that close by was a pit where possibly Dervacus once lay. Beyond that, nothing is known for sure of the identity of Dervacus – who he was or where and when he lived. It's a mysterious and evocative stone in the most enigmatic of sites.

From Maen Madoc the Roman road continues south-westwards and drops down to cross the River Nedd before climbing back up through woods to continue its progress towards Coelbren and Neath. Although there are pockets of urbanization and industry further south, most of the route is highly scenic and can be followed along public rights of way.

The Romans at Brecon

After a lonely passage through the remote hills, the Romans' military road from Neath eventually crossed the River Usk to link with a fort just to the west of present-day Brecon. Only a small part of Y Gaer has been exposed and the site has not been developed for visitors; to reach it on foot you must first ask permission from the local landowner. However, some of the finds from the site can be seen at Brecknock Museum, located in the centre of Brecon, and where there are three floors of fascinating exhibits from all eras of Brecon's history. The Roman items include a tombstone called the Maiden's Stone (Maen y Morwynion) depicting a man and his wife in an embrace. The inscription explains that it was a memorial erected by his wife, and was found near Y Gaer in the 1500s.

There's also a Roman military tombstone for a cavalry trooper stationed at Y Gaer, which like the previous one was recovered from a Roman cemetery near the fort. The Vettonian Spanish cavalry regiment was believed to be the first to occupy Y Gaer. Like the Dalmatian

cohort posted to Hardknott fort in Cumbria (see pages 132-9), they were a 500-strong unit of auxiliaries. The inscription on the stone reads: 'To the spirits of the departed [and] of Candidus' and records that the 20-year-old man had seen just three years' service. Later the fort was rebuilt either under the directions of or actually by members of the 2nd Augustan Legion from Caerleon, since their stamp regularly appears on stonework found at the site.

Other items recovered from the fort, mostly during excavations carried out by Sir Mortimer Wheeler during the 1920s, include everyday Roman items such as beads and spoons, bone dice and gaming counters, a small bronze pendant and brooch, plus a few items of Samian tableware produced in central and southern Gaul (France) and imported until the 3rd century. These attractive red pots and bowls often had their maker's name stamped on the underside, and bore elaborate designs. They would have been used not by the rank and file but by the commanding officers.

Gold-diggers

The six Roman roads that radiated out of Brecon included a major route south from the legionary fortress at Caerleon, and after Brecon this continued to Llandovery and Carmarthen. From Llandovery the Roman road passed the gold mine at Dolaucothi, the only known one in Roman Britain, and no doubt important for the minting of coins. The gold-bearing pyrites were dug from underground galleries and extracted from opencast workings, and although the landscape has been altered following further mining in the 19th and early 20th centuries, it is still possible to make out where a reservoir was fashioned to provide water for blasting and washing the ore. A fragment of wooden water wheel dating from Roman times has even been found at the site. The mines are now in the hands of the National Trust, which has established an interpretative display, waymarked walks and even holds gold-panning sessions.

ABOVE: the Romans' fort of Y Gaer was once an important hub in a network of strategic routes.

PEDDARS WAY

IN THE HEART OF EAST ANGLIA

Many of our foremost Roman roads are today covered with tarmac and echo to the sound of the motorcar, but there is a well-preserved Roman route in north-west Norfolk that you can still explore on foot and which offers a peaceful passage through the gentlest of rural landscapes. The Peddars Way remains a fine example of Roman engineering, and was probably built after Boudicca's revolt to subdue the Iceni. However, where it originally went and why is a question that continues to puzzle historians. From Roman road to National Trail, the Peddars Way offers the perfect opportunity to step out with the legions and experience a march — or stroll, if you prefer — along an authentic Roman highway.

The Peddars Way, together with the Norfolk Coast Path, forms a 93-mile (150km) walking route through East Anglia that begins at Knettishall Heath, near Thetford in Suffolk, and heads roughly north-west towards the mouth of the Wash. It's a designated official long-distance footpath, called a National Trail, and its route is efficiently indicated by acorn waymarks, as well as by standard finger posts; plus there are several guidebooks, a list of accommodation providers and a very useful official website with a large amount of up to date information with which to plan your trip (see information panel). This includes details of village services, pubs and cafe along the way, a distance chart and even GPS data. Local bus timetables can also be downloaded, with services connecting the start and finish of the walk via King's Lynn.

Links With the Past

Although the Peddars Way National Trail officially begins in Suffolk, the surviving Roman road really gets into its stride north of Castle Acre. From this point it heads straight as a die to the coast at Holme next the Sea and, apart from the first couple of miles, it is virtually all off road on pleasant paths and tracks across a gentle and undemanding landscape. Before you start the walk do visit Castle Acre, a picturesque village that was once possibly an Iceni settlement and later a Roman encampment. Today, the remains of an 11th-century priory and castle are the most visible links with the past, the castle including the huge western gateway that was the outer entrance of the original bailey.

Our walk begins just off the Peddars Way at the village of Great Massingham, where the bus stop, post office stores and handsome 15th-century Church of St Mary sit comfortably side-by-side overlooking the huge green. Walk round the far side of the pond and out past Summerwood Estate,

PEDDARS WAY, NORFOLK

Start: Great Massingham, GR 797229
Finish: Holme next the Sea, GR 696439
Distance: 16 miles/25.5km
Time: 6–7 hours
Terrain: Easy and mostly flat, including farm tracks and grassy field edges, with some potentially muddy stretches
Map: OS Explorer 250: Norfolk Coast West
Guidebooks: *Peddars Way & Norfolk Coast Path National Trail Guide* by Bruce Robinson (Aurum Press); *Norfolk Origins 3: Celtic Fire and Roman Rule* by Robinson & Gregory (Poppyland Publishing); *A Norfolk Songline* by Hugh Lapton (Hickathrift Books – available from National Trail Office); *The Boudiccan Revolt against Rome* by Paul Sealey (Shire Archaeology)
Public transport: Both the start of the work (Great Massingham) and finish (Holme next the Sea) are served by buses from King's Lynn. For details of routes and timetables go to www.travelineeastanglia.org.uk or www.passengertransport.norfolk.gov.uk
Information: King's Lynn Tourist Information Centre 01553 763044; Swaffham Tourist Information Centre 01760 722255; Peddars Way & Norfolk Coast Path National Trail Office 01328 850530; www.nationaltrail.co.uk/peddarsway

ABOVE: The remains of the 11th-century priory at Castle Acre, near the start of the walk.

THE FIRST ROAD-BUILDERS

So, what did the Romans ever do for us? Well, the most obvious answer is they gave us our first national road network. Of course, roads in a general sense existed before the Romans came along, but on the whole they were a series of unplanned and unsurfaced tracks. The Romans laid out a methodical, organized system linking their key settlements and forts and, thanks to sophisticated surveying techniques, they stuck to as straight a course as possible between destinations so that their troops could move fast and efficiently to wherever they were needed. Altogether the Romans built an estimated 10,000 miles of roads in Britain — although the true figure may be much higher, since some routes have almost certainly been lost to time.

Another reason there is so much respect for their work is that their road-building techniques were highly developed. The average Roman road would have a deep, solid foundation of large stones, topped in Norfolk's case by a mix of flint, gravel, small stones and clay mixed into a hard consistency and rammed down; elsewhere, the surface might be finished with paving stones. Good drainage was paramount, and often this was achieved by raising the road on a bank or causeway called an 'agger', as can still be seen on the Peddars Way between Anmer and Fring (and also on Stane Street on top of the South Downs — see page 107). The size of the agger varied from road to road, just as the material used in the road's construction depended on what was locally available. Either way, routes such as the Peddars Way were the motorways of their day, and their legacy endures.

BELOW: 'A Norfolk Songline' celebrates the Peddars Way through a series of modern sculptures and poems.

forking left onto a concrete farm track past the unavoidable transmitter mast to reach the Peddars Way. Turn right, and follow this all the way to the coast.

Immediately you will be struck by several things, some of which will be obvious. First, the Peddars Way really is very straight. The Roman engineers didn't meet any serious obstacles between here and the coast (such as major rivers or hills) so apart from the occasional slight shift, the route kept straight and true and wasted little time deviating. Second, it's also quite broad, and although successive users, including today's modern farm and recreation vehicles, may have widened it a little, it shows that even supposedly minor or fringe Roman roads were still constructed to exacting standards and were never simply 'paths' as we understand the term today. The third impression, and this one might creep up on you slowly, is that away from the main roads and the coast, the gentle countryside of Norfolk is surprisingly quiet and empty of people, which generally makes for a peaceful walk. (It also means that there probably won't be anyone looking when you play Romans versus Iceni with your children in the hedgerows after lunch.)

'A Norfolk Songline'

Since route-finding along the Peddar's Way is ridiculously easy, let yourself become immersed in your thoughts and reflect on who has walked this way before and why. This was in the mind of writer Hugh Lupton and sculptor Tom Perkins when they created a series of poems and sculptures along the Peddars Way called A *Norfolk Songline*. You will meet the first of two of their works of art on the stretch at the edge of the path near Little Massingham. It's a large tablet of stone next to some woodland, inscribed with a short and evocative poem that looks to capture the spirit of the land — not just its raw materials, but how since early times man has interacted with the landscape through farming, settlement and its thoroughfares. These lines of communication are all-important, and Songlines explores how the Romans straightened the 'old tangled trackways' of the Celtic tribes and straightened them into an 'efficient military artery' throughout East Anglia. It also challenges us, as modern walkers, to pause, look at the ground at our feet and consider how momentary and short-lived are our footprints, and how many other pairs of feet must have gone before us.

Cross the A148 by the boarding kennels at Harpley Dams and continue along the wide, hedged thoroughfare. The thickets are usually alive with small birds, such as chaffinches and great tits, while yellowhammers and linnets flit between the fields. Skylarks are a constant companion in the sky above, trilling away for all they're worth, and you might see the occasional partridge scuttling about the fields. Inevitably, at some point or other, you will startle a pheasant (more likely it will startle you), and their ubiquitous seed bins are testimony to the fact that these birds – originally introduced from Asia – are largely bred for shooting.

Romans versus Iceni

It is quite possible that the marching Roman soldiers would have been eyeing the undergrowth with some wariness, too, but for entirely different reasons. The Iceni were a Teutonic tribe who settled in Britain around 200 BC, and from their strongholds in northern Norfolk they initially sided with the Romans. But after the death of Iceni King

BELOW: Through the heart of the Norfolk countryside – the Peddars Way near Great Massingham.

LEFT: The stuff of legends – Queen Boudicca on her famous chariot leads the Iceni revolt against the Romans.

BELOW: Wooden defences at the recreated Iceni village at Cockley Cley, near Swaffham.

Prasutagus, Queen Boudicca led a revolt (around AD 60–61) and with an army of over 120,000 sacked Colchester, St Albans and London, and very nearly succeeded in bringing an end to Roman rule in Britain. As it was, the Romans' superior tactical and fighting skills triumphed, despite inferior numbers. The Iceni were crushed and Boudicca, we are led to believe, ended up taking her own life. Despite that, she appears to live on as something of a national heroine, and you can discover more about her and experience a fully recreated Iceni settlement at Iceni Village, open daily (April–October), at Cockley Cley, near Swaffham.

The upshot of the Iceni revolt, on the part of the Romans, was a determined and ruthless purge of the Iceni heartland, and to do this they extended their systematic road system throughout East Anglia. Peddars Way was one of several new routes that criss-crossed the region, probably finished some time around AD 70. However, the name itself is not believed to be Roman. It probably dates from the last few hundred years and most likely refers to a thoroughfare used by those travelling on foot or carrying goods (pedlars).

Before and After the Romans

As the track opens out on Harpley Common you will notice a large tumulus across to the right, and there is a second further ahead which is very close to the path.

These remind us that Norfolk was inhabited long before the Romans and Iceni; indeed, the ancient Icknield Way that ran across the broad chalk ridge to the west was used as far back as Neolithic times. The tumuli are Bronze Age burial mounds; while other relics of the past have been found nearby at Snettisham, where priceless gold torcs (heavy, twisted rings worn around the neck as symbols of wealth and power) and other remarkable Iron Age remains have been unearthed in the last 50 years.

Beyond the woods to the east, much more recent history is celebrated at Houghton Hall, one-time residence of Sir Robert Walpole, the 18th-century Whig politician who is generally considered Britain's first prime minister. Now the residence of Lord and Lady Cholmondeley, the elegant neo-Palladian hall and spacious grounds are open to the public from April to September on Wednesdays, Thursdays and Sundays.

Once across a couple of roads you pass a wildlife conservation area, but despite this the overwhelming impression is of a highly developed agricultural landscape. Even as far back as Roman times, when East Anglia would have been a mix of wild heath and woodland, not to mention the watery fenland out to the west, early farmers would have made their mark on the land, clearing small areas for basic crops and grazing stock, and using paths to link scattered communities. Fast-forward two thousand years and you can see how intensively these rich soils are now worked, but by how few people! One relic of the past is the windmill at Great Bircham, its huge white sails in view away to the right. This tower mill was built in 1846 and, now restored to working order, it is open to the public daily from Easter to September. You can climb up to the fan deck at the top and admire the views, while on ground level there's a tearoom and bakery (where bread is freshly baked most days).

The Peddars Way continues to cut a solitary and at time quite remote route across the landscape. Copses and small woods dot the immense, open fields, and every now and then you spy a solitary tractor labouring away in the distance. There's the odd farmhouse or cottage, and an occasional glimpse of a hamlet or village, such as Anmer, Great Bircham

ABOVE: Daily life at the Iceni village includes period dress, cooking and all the humble chores necessary to keep an Iron Age settlement going.

and Fring, but apart from pubs and post office stores at Great Bircham and Sedgeford it isn't until Ringstead that you meet any shop on the actual route – so make sure to pack a picnic. Not that the Roman soldiers would be dallying, for as the coast gets ever closer they would be making good progress. And it's on this open stretch near Fring that some of the best surviving sections of the Roman road can be seen. In places, the track is as much as 30 to 40 feet (9 to 12m) wide and runs up to 2 feet (6.5m) above the surroundings fields on a raised bank known as an agger. The agger not only afforded good drainage but also allowed the marching soldiers a view of the surrounding land and possible attacks.

Lavender Fields

Although just off the route, the estate village of Fring is an attractive little place, with a 14th-century church and, like so many villages in these parts, a number of beautiful flint-and-brick buildings. It was also once the centre of Norfolk's lavender industry, which survives at Caley Mill, near Heacham, the oldest lavender farm in Britain and home to the

ABOVE: The 19th-century tower mill at Great Bircham is visible from the Peddars Way.

National Collection of Lavenders. Although not conclusively proven, it is believed that the Romans introduced the herb to Britain as part of their medicinal or perhaps culinary supplies, and although Norfolk's beds are much reduced, they still produce a wonderful summertime spectacle around Heacham and Sandringham to the west of the Peddars Way.

Ever so gradually the land becomes more undulating, and beyond Fring Cross on the lane to Sedgeford you are treated to what passes for a hill in north Norfolk – although it's barely 200 feet (60m) above sea level and sadly doesn't appear to have a name. The trail emerges on the B1454 by Littleport Cottages, a delightful terraced row that variously incorporates flint, brick, pebble-dash and wood in its construction. Across the road the Peddars Way proceeds along the drive past Magazine Cottage, a curious, hexagonal building that looks like an old school house or chapel. It was built in 1642 by Sir Hamon le Strange, the Royalist Governor of King's Lynn, and its name – plus its curious semi-basement – reflects its use as an arms depot or armoury, although it also incorporated a small gaol.

A little beyond Magazine Farm, the Peddars Way crosses the former Heacham–Wells railway line before cresting a small rise and dropping down to become the surfaced 'Peddars

Way South' into the houses of Ringstead. Follow the pavement round to the left and onto the High Street past the Gin Trap, the 17th-century village pub named after the cruel (and now illegal) steel trap once used to trap the leg of an animal – or human. Food is served lunchtime and evening, and the well-stocked post office stores opposite (which includes an antiques centre) also sells refreshments. Next to the pub is Ringstead Gallery, housed in the former stable block, which since 1974 has put on ever-changing shows of paintings, bronzes, ceramics and turned wood.

Down to the Sea
After 13 miles or so (about 22km) of Roman footslogging throgh East Anglia you will probably be in need of refuelling. However, the end is almost in sight with Norfolk's north coast just over the hill ahead. To

RIGHT: The peaceful village of Fring was once an important centre for the growing of lavender, a herb reputedly introduced to Britain by the Romans.

BELOW: This beautiful old barn at Fring is typical of the flint and brick buildings that seem to sit so naturally in the Norfolk countryside.

RIGHT: the end of the road – the Romans' highway through Norfolk ends among the sand dunes at Holme next the Sea, near Hunstanton.

reach the sea continue along the pavement, leaving Ringstead by the appropriately named 'Peddars Way North'. Just past the sail-less former windmill, take a signposted footpath across the fields and down towards the shimmering blue sea. Go straight over the A149 and along Beach Road opposite. The centre of Holme next the Sea, where the White Horse serves food and drink daily, is off Westgate Road on the right; otherwise continue to the far end of the lane where there is a seasonal refreshments kiosk and toilet block by the car park. Unless you are being met, the bus stop is back on the main road, or you can continue for a further couple of miles westwards into Hunstanton (the official path leaves the lane further back) from where there are frequent buses into King's Lynn.

Looking seawards, on the far side of the golf course, is Holme Dunes Nature Reserve, a fittingly dramatic conclusion to your Roman odyssey across Norfolk. The Wildlife Trust's visitor centre is away to the right, reached via the Norfolk Coast Path which now takes over at this point and wriggles its way round the vast saltmarshes and mudflats, golden beaches and low-lying pasture that is such a haven for wildlife.

However, that's an adventure for another day. For now, it's time to unbuckle those leather sandals, cast off shield and sword and put down your heavy load, and maybe like the Roman troops before you, wander across the dunes to dip your hot feet in the cool waters of the North Sea. Here is perhaps the best place to address a question that may have been nagging at you for most of the walk, or even when you first set eyes on the map: why does a major, 50-mile Roman road simply end near an insignificant village on the north Norfolk coast? No one knows for certain, but it is suggested that there might have been a

ferry to the far side of the Wash from this point; or perhaps there was an anchorage for vessels? There was certainly a Roman fort at Brancaster (*Branodunum*), a few miles along the coast, although it seems likely that it was built some time after the road was constructed. It once more brings us back to a central theme of the Peddars Way, namely that for the Romans it almost certainly had symbolic value as well as practical value. It allowed troops to get around the natives' heartland quickly and easily, but it was also a powerful visible message to the insubordinate Iceni that the Romans were in control and were here to stay. Ironically, of course, they didn't; yet many centuries later we're still walking along their remarkable road.

DERE STREET

AGRICOLA'S WILD AND WINDSWEPT ROAD

It's tempting to imagine that, like our modern motorway network, the major Roman roads were largely lowland corridor routes that connected major towns. This may have been the case in much of southern and central England, where the likes of Watling Street and the Fosse Way crossed the Midlands, but as we discover elsewhere in this book, the Romans became engaged in a protracted military campaign to subdue the native tribes of Wales and Scotland, and they needed a fast and effective means of sending troops and supplies to the battle zone. The fine hill walk featured here follows a stunning section of the Romans' Dere Street across the wild and windswept Cheviot Hills, high on the English/Scottish border. The challenging terrain and sheer remoteness of the location is testimony to the ambition and expertise of the Roman road-builders, for whom the small matter of a chain of 1,500-feet hills (450m) was no obstacle.

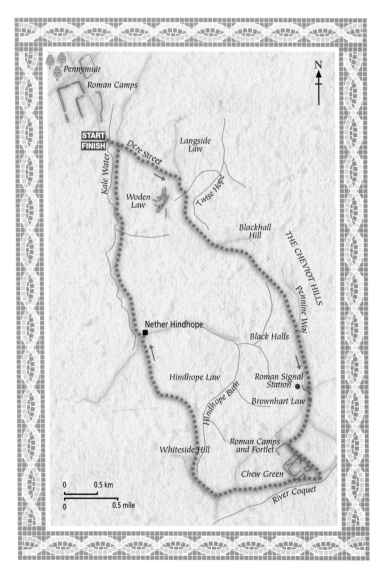

This walk explores a section of Dere Street across the top of the Cheviots, a range of unpopulated Northumbrian hills whose rugged beauty is matched only by their height and remoteness. It's a scenic and invigorating hill walk, but as with any such outing you must be properly equipped and armed with the relevant Ordnance Survey map; note that the ground can be wet and boggy in places.

The outing begins near the grassy remains of the Romans' temporary marching camps at Pennymuir. The largest of these covered 42 acres (17ha) and could have accommodated over 1,000 men (two legions). It's remarkably well preserved, and in places the ramparts are nearly 4 feet (1.25m) high. Marching camps were just that – places where the troops rested as they progressed along a route. Here it was Dere Street, and such was the importance of this south–north Roman road into Scotland that as many as 14 separate marching camps (probably dating from and used at different times) have been identified in just a 20-mile stretch of the route near the present Scottish border. The camps offered security and shelter, and usually consisted of rudimentary defences featuring earth ramparts topped with a wooden palisade; a ditch would be dug around the outer edge. Although the specifications of the camp could vary according to the terrain, the layout followed a standard pattern with the leather tents erected in set rows (very much like the ordered layout of other Roman military defences) so that the camp could be erected and dismantled swiftly. The Roman soldiers were adept at more than just marching and fighting, of course.

DERE STREET, CHEVIOT HILLS

Start & finish: Grassy pull-off by Kale Water, near Pennymuir Roman camp, GR 761134
Distance: 9½ miles/15km
Time: 5–6 hours
Terrain: Rough and exposed hillside, with some long slopes and boggy patches
Map: OS Outdoor Leisure 16: Cheviot Hills
Guidebooks: None
Public transport: None
Information: Jedburgh Tourist Information Centre 0870 6080404

There is limited roadside parking at Pennymuir, so it is probably best to drive on down the unfenced lane a little further and park on the open grassy verge where the road fords Kale Water. If you have already inspected Pennymuir, or are leaving it to the end, begin the walk by crossing the river on the footbridge next to the ford and continue up the lane on the other side (heading eastwards). At the junction of roads at the top, go over the stile ahead and up across the sloping field. A sign on the adjoining gate reminds users that Dere Street is a Scheduled Ancient Monument and there is no right of access for motorized vehicles.

BELOW: The marching camp at Pennymuir, near the start of the walk, was large enough to accommodate two legions on the move.

Exploring Dere Street

Dere Street was a major Roman artery into Scotland, a vital line of communication, trade and military support. For a long time it was known as Agricola's Road, since it was almost certainly built following Agricola's initial push into Scotland around AD 80–81 – and as such pre-dates Hadrian's Wall. Because of the Romans' ever-changing plans for their northern frontier (see the Antonine Wall walk, page 150), the envisaged road network covering southern Scotland never fully materialized, and Dere Street remained the key Roman road that connected northern England (and later Hadrian's Wall) with Scotland. It ran from York, headquarters of the 9th Legion (see page 78), to finish on the Forth near Edinburgh. North of Hadrian's Wall, in particular, the course of the former Roman military road is still plainly evident today. The modern A68 follows it northwards between Corbridge and High Rochester on long switchback sections that are unwavering (and breathtaking) in their straightness. Even after the Romans left, Dere Street continued to be well used and served as the main route between England and Scotland until as recently as the late 1700s, when a new road over Carter Bar was engineered. However, in one of those neat twists of fate, much of the former Roman military road across the Northumberland hills is still used by today's army, which trains in the vast Otterburn range. Incidentally, the name 'Dere Street' is believed to have been coined in the Middle Ages and, like Sarn Helen (see page 12), was probably known differently to the Romans.

From the lane, slant up across the rough pasture towards the wall on your right. Cross another stile, then with the wall on your left continue along the clear and obvious bumpy track (Dere Street) uphill. Approaching the top the route eventually bears right, past a stone shelter and animal enclosure, and, as the gradient levels out, follow the well-used track across the hilltop with glorious views eastwards over the bare and open Cheviot Hills. These uplands are not harsh and craggy, like those of the Lake District or Scottish Highlands, but smooth and rounded, and yet their height and remoteness make them a hillwalker's paradise. The Cheviots

BELOW: One of numerous earth ramparts and seige lines built by the Romans on the ancient hillfort of Woden Law.

occupy the northern end of the Northumberland National Park, and away to the north-east culminate in the 2,676 feet (815m) summit of the Cheviot itself. Although there are areas of heather, bracken and bilberry, these are not managed grouse moors along the lines of the North York Moors, Peak District or some of the Scottish Highlands. Instead, centuries of grazing have left them clothed mainly in rough grasses, although in the boggier area you will see plenty of sphagnum moss and the wispy white buds of cotton grass bending in the wind.

Woden Law Hillfort

If you study the Ordnance Survey maps, you will see that many of the surrounding hilltops are crowned with ancient hillforts that pre-date the Romans. One such is Woden Law, whose broad grassy summit is now over the brow to your right. If you want to nip up the slope and inspect the site there's a crossing point in the fence towards the top or a small gate a little further on, but as with many of these places there isn't too much to see on the ground today, save a few grassy ditches and ramparts.

Although Woden Law provided a defensive position for local tribes long before Agricola's troops arrived, the Romans strengthened it by adding two new banks and three ditches. Excavations have revealed that the outer bank was flat-topped and reinforced, probably to support Roman catapult machines. But the fort also bears outlines of other isolated and puzzlingly incomplete earthworks, most of which appear to have little defensive value. One theory is that they were constructed by the Roman troops stationed at nearby Pennymuir as part of their training, including practice siege works, and that in fact Woden Law had little real strategic significance for the Romans.

Where the wall on your left falls away, go straight on along a clear grassy track (not the one downhill to the left), maintaining your height and enjoying the expansive views from the high grassy ridge. In the narrow valley far below to your left, containing a stream called Twise Hope, is a circular stone sheepfold, one of several you will see today. Sheepfolds

THE ROMAN ROAD NETWORK

Although Dere Street was the Romans' main route from northern England into Scotland, it was just one of a huge network of roads that the Romans wasted no time in laying across their newly conquered territory. Of course, these carefully plotted routes helped the swift deployment of troops and equipment and allowed good communications, but they also served to reinforce among the local population the perception of Roman dominance. Despite many new roads being built from scratch, the Roman surveyors and engineers were also happy to use existing routes (albeit with a little straightening up!), such as the ancient Icknield Way, which ran across southern England into East Anglia. Initially the roads were designed with the military in mind, but over the years they often ended up becoming important civilian and trading routes. Despite falling into neglect after the Romans left, many of their principal routes are still in use today. For instance, much of Watling Street, a major Roman road connecting Richborough and the Channel ports with Wroxeter via London, is now the A2 and A5; the Romans' former trans-Pennine route through the Stainmore Gap is today known to most drivers as the A66, and Dere Street's arrow-like progress across the Northumbrian countryside (outlined in this chapter) forms part of the modern A68. Other Roman roads that have also passed down into history, not to mention our road atlases, include Ermine Street between London and York, the Fosse Way (Exeter, Cirencester, Leicester and Lincoln – see pages 98–99) and Akeman Street, connecting St Albans and Cirencester. For further reading on this absorbing subject see *In the Footsteps of Caesar: Walking Roman Roads in Britain* by Helen Livingstone (Dial House, 1995).

ABOVE: Dere Street reaches 1,600ft (500m) at Brownhart Law, where the Romans maintained a signal station.

are simply small pens or enclosures built on the hillside and used by shepherds to temporarily hold the animals.

Soon you arrive at a gate bearing a helpful sign ('Dere Street, Chew Green') and a clear path beyond. The original Roman road may have taken a slightly higher course from here, but this waymarked route below Blackhall Hill's western face is a better and probably easier option for today's walker. Although there are occasional patches of scree, the path across the slope is straightforward and there are lovely views down the valley. After a long and gradual climb the path finally reaches the summit ridge at Black Halls, where a signpost by a gate announces the meeting point of Dere Street and the Pennine Way.

The Pennine Way National Trail is Britain's oldest long-distance footpath, opened in 1965 and stretching all the way from Edale in the Peak District to Kirk Yetholm in Scotland – about 17 miles north from here. If you encounter any determined-looking backpackers heading purposefully towards you at this point, bear in mind that they may well have set off on their own walk not from the valley below but from Derbyshire, over 230 miles (370km) to the south, so give them an encouraging nod at the least.

Dere Street and the Pennine Way now join forces for just under 2 miles, so beyond the gate head southwards with the English–Scottish border fence on your right (follow signs for Chew Green). Away to your left is the vast Otterburn military training range, and when manoeuvres are taking place you will see red flags flying and may even hear the occasional boom of heavy artillery being put through their paces. Needless to say, this walk is entirely outside the range and you are perfectly safe.

Continue over the brow of Brownhart Law, the site of a Roman signal station. These small constructions usually consisted of a wooden or sometimes stone tower, surrounded by an earth rampart and ditch. The tower incorporated a platform from which the messages would be relayed by a variety of means, including fire (beacons) and smoke or, if the stations were close enough, by flag.

Ignore various footpaths and bridleways off left and right, including one for a long-distance bridleway route called the Border Ride, and continue on the purposeful track southwards across the wild and open grassy hillside. Eventually you dip down to cross a stream called Chew Sike via a wooden footbridge and some newly laid flagstones (a counter-erosion measure); on the far bank is Chew Green marching camp.

The Camp in the Hills

The outer boundary of the Romans' camp is today denoted by curious, star-shaped metal posts. Turn left and follow the Pennine Way – still the course of Dere Street – downhill to inspect the heart of the camp, where, among the jumble of ditches and grassy ramparts, the remains of a small, square fortlet is the most visible of the surviving defences.

There is no modern interpretation at Chew Green – no panels with maps or artists' impressions of what it might have looked like, not even any signposts, save a few marker posts. Instead, you have to visualize how the small encampment must have spread over the barren hillside. An understanding of the site is not helped by the fact that the maze of grassy walls and ditches date from different times, leaving a confusing pattern. The original camp was established around AD 80–81 for Roman soldiers travelling along Dere Street, and about a century later a further encampment was added, followed by the construction of a fortlet. Chew Green was designed to house a permanent detachment of troops (it was originally intended to be big enough for a whole legion), who would police the exposed stretches of Dere Street and offer protection for the regular convoys of supplies and equipment heading north to the Romans' frontier in Scotland.

Carry on down the slope below the camp towards the infant River Coquet, with an open, surfaced road visible on the opposite hillside. At a signpost turn right for the Pennine Way (and not the Coquet Valley, indicated left) and follow this grassy route westwards above sheep enclosures and up on to higher ground. On the skyline far ahead is a dark green strip of conifers, while behind you the grassy borders of the marching camp are now quite

ABOVE: Bare and remote – the ditches and banks of the Romans' camp at Chew Green, on the roof of the Cheviots.

ABOVE LEFT: A new footbridge and paved path are designed to counter the boggy conditions aroud Chew Sike.

distinctive. Continue across the featureless hilltop with occasional posts indicating the route until you reach a fence, and, waving goodbye to the Pennine Way, turn right. With the fence on your left, follow this unwaymarked track through a gate, after which it bears half-right (north) away from the fence and below the summit of Whiteside Hill, with Hindhope Burn below to your right. The route – a wide and clear grassy track – now bounds downhill across the gentle, open hillside, with glorious views ahead towards Blackhall Hill and your high-level route from earlier. Instead of climbing back up towards Hindhope Law (immediately ahead), the track swings left and down towards a small plantation. Here it turns right, on a much clearer farm track, and descends to the farmstead of Nether Hindhope. Go left on to the drive and then right on to the quiet and open lane in the valley bottom above the meandering Kale Water. Return along this back to the start.

North of Pennymuir and the Cheviot Hills, Dere Street continues across the low farmland east of Jedburgh, ultimately heading for the banks of the Forth near Edinburgh. Initially its wide and direct route is extremely well preserved, sometimes as minor roads but more often as an accessible and signposted walking route. It is depicted by waymarks bearing a Roman helmet, and some of it forms the basis of the St Cuthbert's Way, a 100-mile (60-km) long-distance footpath between Melrose and Lindisfarne in Northumberland that traces locations associated with the legendary saint. However, Melrose is also close to where Dere Street changes direction to visit a large fort at Newstead (*Trimontium*). Although nothing visible remains of it, the base once provided vital support for the Antonine Wall further north (see page 150), and today's visitor can learn much about its history at the Three Hills Roman Heritage Centre in Melrose. The centre features exhibitions and artefacts surrounding daily life on Roman's Scottish frontier, including replica Roman costumes, Arrius's altar to Diana and Scotland's only Roman milestone. There are also afternoon guided walks to the site of the fort – for more details go to www.trimontium.net.

Bremenium Roman Fort

To the south of Chew Green, Dere Street continues across the Northumbrian hills, and from the hamlet of High Rochester to the Romans' base at Corbridge, near Hadrian's Wall, the route is more or less along the line of the modern A68. However, at High Rochester the Romans also established a permanent fort, known as *Bremenium*, and today you can visit the remains of this key staging post. In fact, it is claimed that *Bremenium* was at one time the most northerly occupied fort in the entire Roman Empire. When the Romans retreated from the Antonine Wall and gave up on their second major foray into Scotland, they fell back to Hadrian's earlier defence across northern England. *Bremenium* then became a key outpost in the buffer zone between the Romans and the hostile tribes to the north – a sort of early-warning station, as the official National Park leaflet to the site helpfully describes it. The remains of the fort are reached after an easy 20-minute walk from the main road. At the beginning of the walk, and managed separately from the fort, is an archaeological visitor centre called *Brigantium* (after the native tribe, the Brigantes, who were such a thorn in the side of the Romans). A collection of reconstructed monuments and buildings attempts to bring ancient British history to life, and it includes a recreated section of the Romans' Dere Street, complete with earthen burial mounds that represent the findings from a nearby Roman cemetery. One of the monumental tombs discovered alongside Dere Street has been estimated at 15 feet (4.5m) high and probably marked the final resting place of an important Roman officer.

BELOW: A Roman helmet on display at Three Hills Roman Heritage Centre in Melrose, Scotland.

ABOVE: Remains of the Romans' fort of Bremenium, near High Rochester, at one time the most northerly occupied fort in the entire Empire.

LEFT: A reconstructed fortified farmstead from the Romano-British period at Brigantium archaeological visitor centre.

ROMAN TOWNS

To the Romans' developed and organized minds, towns played a crucial role. They were the political and administrative nerve centre, a market place and focus for craftsmen and professionals, plus they also gave so-called 'client kings' and native people a measure of autonomy – but strictly on the Romans' terms. Some towns were well-defended, in particular the legionary garrisons from where the Romans exercised their military control over the new province of Britannia. Above all, though, towns were civilized and ordered places, with a methodical street system and clearly-defined layout. In Roman Silchester and St Albans you can see the birth of our modern town halls and open squares, shopping parades, public baths and sewerage systems. Urban planning effectively began with the Romans.

OPPOSITE: Constantine the Great was proclaimed Emperor by his troops while in York. Today, his fine and imperious statue gazes down on visitors to the Minster.

SILCHESTER

TRACING A VANISHED TOWN

The Roman town of Calleva Atrebatum (Silchester) takes its name from a local Iron Age tribe, the Atrebates, who had a small settlement here in the gentle, wooded countryside of northern Hampshire between modern-day Reading and Basingstoke. Late in the 1st century AD the Romans chose Silchester as their administrative base for the region, and maps show a network of routes radiating out to the likes of Winchester, St Albans and London. However, when the Romans packed up and left for good less than five centuries later, the town was completely abandoned, and the once-thriving settlement decayed and disappeared beneath the fields and copses. Silchester, like Wroxeter in Shropshire and Caistor in Norfolk, shares the distinction of having never been built on subsequently, so that today only the well-preserved walls and tree-lined amphitheatre give any indication of its former life. It makes for a peaceful and extremely evocative setting, full of atmosphere, where you can wander largely undisturbed and turn your thoughts back two millennia.

The walk begins at the large visitor car park to the north of the site of the deserted town (not the small car park by the church). The modern village of Silchester is a mile or so away, so follow the prominent road signs for 'Roman Silchester'. There is a waymarked Roman Town Trail around the entire walled perimeter, about 1½ miles (2.4km) long, and which is coincidental to some of our route. Handy information panels dot this route, and the first of these is in the corner of the car park, from where a short fenced path leads to the wall itself.

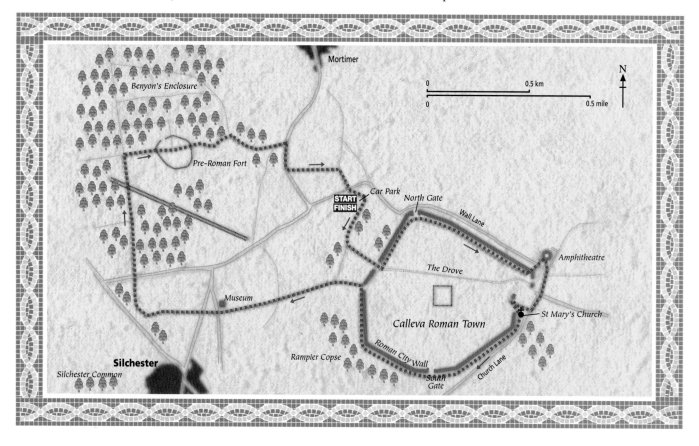

SILCHESTER, HAMPSHIRE

Start & finish: Roman Silchester public car park, GR 636629
Distance: 4½ miles/7km
Time: 3–4 hours
Terrain: Unsurfaced field paths and woodland tracks, some of which may be muddy after wet weather
Map: OS Explorer 159: Reading, Wokingham & Pangbourne
Guidebooks: *A Guide to Silchester* by Michael Fulford (Calleva Museum); *Roman Town Trail –* leaflet (free)
Public transport: Bus 143 runs from Reading to Silchester Common, near the walk, while Mortimer station is 2 miles away (trains from Reading)
Information: Reading Tourist Information Centre 0118 956 6226; www.silchester.rdg.ac.uk

BELOW: The Roman walls of Silchester are among the best preserved in the whole of Britain.

ABOVE: Academics lead annual digs at Silchester, and public involvement is encouraged.

BELOW: Silchester is one of very few sites in Roman Britain that was not subsequently built upon, and is thus a valuable historical resource.

When you reach a junction of tracks there is a wide and open bridleway ahead, known as The Drove, which cuts across the middle of the broad site. Ignore this tempting route and instead turn sharply left, and go through a kissing gate for the path either beside or on top of the town's former wall. As you begin to trace the boundary of Silchester, or *Calleva*, look over to the right. This was the heart of a bustling 107-acre (43-ha) settlement, complete with streets and buildings, which in its heyday may have supported a population of several thousand. Today there is nothing but open fields. Apart from waymarked rights of way such as The Drove, public access is not permitted to the central area, which is leased out as farmland and carefully managed. Mind you, at first glance there's not too much to see, given that the town was deserted almost 2,000 years ago.

The first proper excavations took place in the late 1800s, when the Society of Antiquaries uncovered a grid system of streets and numerous buildings. There were temples and a bathhouse, plus the usual basilica and forum at the centre of the settlement. Most of the key finds are incorporated in what is known as the Silchester Collection at Reading Museum, and if your itinerary allows it is well worth a visit. When the digs were concluded early last century, the Roman town was once more covered up to protect it from the elements, as well as souvenir hunters and vandals.

Since the 1970s, further excavations have been carried out by the University of Reading, and each summer the Department of Archaeology holds a popular field school at the site. Visitors are welcome, with viewing platforms and student-led tours, and there are activity sheets for children and even a 'dig pit' for you to experience the work first hand. One recent dig – the Insula IX Town Life project – has involved the detailed excavation of one specific block of the Roman town – but despite the painstaking work, many of the secrets of Roman Silchester remain buried beneath the soil.

TOWN PLANNING ROMAN-STYLE

Although some Roman towns were built virtually from scratch, others – like Silchester – developed from pre-Roman settlements, and as such underwent wholescale changes in design and layout as the Roman town-planners got to work. Towards the end of the 1st century, the streets of Silchester were re-laid in a grid fashion similar to modern American cities and typical of the Romans' methodical and regimented approach. The resulting network of crossing routes created blocks, called *insulae*, which were often remarkably uniform, and at Silchester most measured roughly 400 x 400 Roman feet. The blocks contained shops and houses, with the central insula occupied by the *forum*. This was the main square or piazza and acted as the civic centre and market place, and it lay at the heart of every Roman settlement. At Silchester, the forum measured 142 x 130 feet (43 x 39m) and was entered via a grand monumental gate. Around three sides was a covered walkway or portico, and on the fourth, opposite the gate, was

the 230 feet (70m) high *basilica*. This imposing building, supported by a row of Corinthian columns, acted as a meeting hall and law court, and was at the administrative centre of the town.

As a 'Romanized' town, Silchester became a regional administrative centre or a *civitas capital*. It elected its own magistrates and town council and as such enjoyed a limited form of self-government. Next step up were the *municipiae*, large provincial towns like St Albans (see pages 50–57), which enjoyed considerable autonomy over matters such as trade, which passed local laws and whose constitution was governed by a charter. Above them were the three *coloniae* of Lincoln, Gloucester and Colchester (see pages 58–67), the highest rank a settlement could achieve. All three had been early Roman military bases and were home to many retired legionaries. The constitution of the *colonia* was modelled on that of Rome's, and its inhabitants were full Roman citizens. The civilian town of York (see pages 58–67) was also later accorded this privilege.

ABOVE: The North Gate, one of four main entrances to the town, was excavated in 1991.

The most visible remains of the Roman town are the encircling walls, of course, and although partly restored and necessarily stabilized in places, they are remarkably well preserved. You can examine them close-up when you arrive at the North Gate, one of four main entrance points, from where a road connected Silchester with Dorchester on Thames. The latter was a Roman town on the River Thames near Shillingford, midway between Cirencester and St Albans, not to be confused with its better-known near-namesake in Dorset, which the Romans called *Durnovaria*. The sketch on the interpretation panel shows what the gatehouse probably looked like, and how solid and imposing it must have appeared. The town's first proper defence was an earthwork rampart erected at some point in the late 2nd century, followed by a stone wall about 100 years later. This systematic rebuilding is typical of Romano-British towns like Silchester, where the layout and design of specific buildings and streets evolved as the Romans asserted their control over existing settlements in the 'client kingdom'. Gradually defences were strengthened, with stone replacing wood, although as the 3rd century wore on this had much to do with protecting Roman interests from mounting local unrest.

After the North Gate the wall veers south-eastwards and there is an impressively long,

straight stretch. Walking along this easy elevated section certainly allows you to appreciate the quality of the craftsmanship, and it also gives you the chance to savour the surrounding countryside. The location was deliberately chosen by both the Iron Age tribesmen and the Romans because of its elevated position on a gravel spur, and today there are attractive pastoral views in every direction. But a walk around the former Roman site is peaceful for another reason. Unlike other Roman towns featured in the book, Silchester was completely abandoned, so that today its setting is quiet and undisturbed – which is all the more remarkable given that it lies between Reading and Basingstoke, close to the busy M4 corridor.

ABOVE: You can walk alongside much of Silchester's original Roman town wall, which, in places, is 15 feet (4.5m) high and almost 9 feet (2.75m) thick.

The Amphitheatre and the Early Church

When the wall ends, go left, via two stiles, to reach the lane. Turn right, and virtually opposite is the entrance to the Roman amphitheatre. Today the high but well-preserved banks are crowned with mature trees, but once this arena held between 4,500 and 9,000 spectators. The amphitheatre (as at Chester) is located just outside the town wall and was constructed soon after the Romans arrived, probably around AD 50, and then rebuilt on several occasions. Apart from the two opposing entrances to the north and south, there are

ABOVE: This small niche in the wall of Silchester's amphitheatre may have housed a shrine.

also recesses in the east and west walls, which may have been tiny shrines.

Leave the amphitheatre by the main gate to turn left on to Wall Lane once more. Immediately the lane bends right, past Manor Farm House — continue along the road (Church Lane) past a junction to reach the Church of St Mary the Virgin. This beautiful medieval building includes the remains of the original font, which suggests that the church dates from the early 1100s. Look out, in particular, for the 16th-century screen featuring a Tudor rose and a pomegranate (badges of Henry VIII and Catherine of Aragon) and the dogtooth ornament above the doorway of the north porch.

However, a much earlier place of Christian worship *may* have been discovered on the site of Silchester Roman town. It is known that two Romano-Celtic temples existed in the town, and that early on the Romans acted swiftly and forcefully to suppress Christian worship in their empire (see the fate of Alban, page 52). But by the time of Emperor Constantine (see York, pages 78–87), attitudes were beginning to change. Excavations at Silchester in 1892 revealed the outline of a small, 4th-century building on the southeast corner of the forum. Measuring just 42 feet (13m) long, with aisles and wings, it includes a tiny patch of surviving mosaic at the base of the apsidal (semi-circular) end. The fragment of mosaic is in a black-and-white chequered pattern and clearly depicts a cross. To the east of the porch is a tiled area, and this could well have been the location for a baptismal font. Because of the general layout, including the east–west position of the building, it was almost certainly a place of worship, and some experts believe it to be a Christian church. If this is true, it may be one of the earliest-known urban Christian churches in northern Europe, and as at Lullingstone (see pages 110–119), indicates the spread of the religion in Britain towards the end of the Roman occupation.

A Walk Along the Wall

Follow the path round the back of the church, the external walls of which incorporate bricks, tiles and masonry taken from the Roman wall and other buildings. Go through the gate on the southern side of the churchyard (between two wooden sheds) and on alongside the town wall. You can either drop down to walk at its foot or follow the route along the top. Both converge at the former South Gate, from where there were roads to the Roman settlements of Chichester and Winchester.

At this point, and if you haven't done so already, you should examine the make-up of the wall itself. Some of this southern section has been partly restored, and from a base almost 9 feet (3m) thick, it stands in places over 15 feet (4.5m) high, so that you can see in detail how it was constructed. Most of the outer, facing stones have long since disappeared, revealing the flint and mortar core. Particularly noticeable are the distinctive layers of rock designed to bond it together and give the wall added strength and stability. These large limestone slabs are believed to have been brought to Silchester from the Bath area, as much as 50 miles away, although the flint probably came from chalk quarried much nearer to the town. In Michael Fulford's authoritative text on Silchester, available locally, he

suggests that as many as 105,000 wagon-loads of flint and 45,000 loads of stones were necessary to build Silchester's mighty walls.

Near the South Gate but inside the actual town, a *mansio* or inn has been identified among the layout of general buildings. It was a two-storeyed house built around a courtyard, and with baths and stables served as a sort of hotel or lodge for Roman officials, in particular for members of the imperial posting service (*cursus publicus*). The town's main bathhouse was also to be found on the south-east side of the settlement, since it was supplied with water from a nearby stream. As usual, it was a large and important building, measuring 141 x 75 feet (43.5 x 23m), systematically adapted over the years.

So what did the inhabitants of this town make or do? Excavations have provided a series of clues. A pile of ox jaws almost certainly means the existence of a tannery, while three

ABOVE: Now partly hidden by vegetation, the Roman amphitheatre once held up to 9,000 spectators and was located just outside the town wall.

cobblers' lasts indicate that leatherworkers were busy here. Hoards of ironwork discovered between 1890 and 1909 include a variety of tools such as tongs, hammers and an anvil, as well as carpenters' tools and agricultural implements including ploughshares. The remains of an iron-smelting furnace have been found, and with parts of barrels suggesting that coopers as well as blacksmiths and bronzesmiths were also at work, the picture is of a busy and productive town supplying and servicing the surrounding rural population.

Beyond the South Gate the path drops down to the foot of the wall, and to your left is Rampier Copse, where a deep, tree-covered ditch and bank are indications of earlier earthwork defences. At a junction of tracks, by the site of the West Gate, turn left. (If you want to shorten the walk, go straight on and left at the next gate, at the end of The Drove, for the path back to the car park.) The long, gated track heads west between fields and finally emerges on a road beside Calleva Museum.

ABOVE: The 12th-century Church of St Mary the Virgin incorporates building material from the original Roman town.

BELOW: More than just a hut – Calleva Museum, ½ mile (800m) from the site of the Roman town.

Museum Piece

Calleva Museum is a wonderful little place, originally opened in 1951 as Silchester's contribution to the Festival of Britain. It's privately run as a charity, and is a green-painted hut that is unstaffed and free to enter. There are photos from excavations, an explanation of what went on in the Roman town, and drawings and models of what it might have looked like.

Another fascinating exhibit is a large aerial photo of Roman Silchester. As you will have seen by now, most of the original town is today managed as farmland, but the growing of crops such as wheat and barley on the site can provide a key to the town's original layout and design. Because the crops cannot root so deeply on the former Roman streets (mostly made of gravel) or along the course of the walls (usually flint), they don't take so long to mature as neighbouring crops that root in deeper, richer and moister ground. This means they are ready for harvest much quicker, and viewed from the air present yellow crop lines against a green background – in effect, a blueprint of the streets, walls and boundaries from Roman times.

So why did the town of Silchester not go on to develop after the Romans left? Why did Salisbury or St Albans grow but Silchester fade and disappear, given its relatively sophisticated urban development and defences? There is no definitive answer, but one possibility is that the emergence of the powerful Anglo-Saxon kingdom of Wessex focused trade and political power on other regional centres, such as Winchester and Dorchester,

such that the pre-eminence of Silchester declined rapidly when the Romans withdrew, and it's possible that the dwindling town was all but abandoned. Medieval occupation of the site, as shown by the establishment of the 12th-century church, occurred significantly later.

To continue the walk, go across the road to the short, unsurfaced lane opposite, then cross another road for a well-used track into the trees, waymarked by a horse-riding symbol. This marks the edge of Silchester Common, and if you are in need of refreshment head left through the silver birches to the sizeable village green, where the appropriately named Calleva Arms public house serves food and drink daily.

However, the main route keeps off the green and passes a primary school on your right. Beyond a distinctive yellow bank of gorse, veer right on the principal track across a small area of open, scrubby common to reach another road. Go straight over, and next to the red-brick house (Heatherbrae) is a wide forest ride indicated 'public footpath'. This peaceful and attractive route heads northwards into Benyon's Inclosure, dominated by mostly Scot's pine in varying stages of development. After ¼ mile (400m), at the wide crossroads of tracks by the noticeboard (and

ABOVE: An aerial view of Roman Silchester, showing excavations past and present.

before your route dips suddenly downhill), turn right. Continue eastwards, through a clearing that marks the site of a pre-Roman fort (the low, outer ramparts are still faintly visible) and down to where the main track bends sharply left towards a lake among the woods. Here go right on a wide track that wriggles its way up among trees and past Little Heath house to the road. Turn right and walk along the edge for about 150m, then cross over for a public footpath indicated down into a copse (full of bluebells in springtime). The path climbs up to a stile, then crosses a field, on the far left-hand side of which is another stile. Go over this and turn right on to a byway. This emerges on Wall Lane opposite the entrance to the Roman Silchester car park.

ST ALBANS

UNCOVERING *VERULAMIUM*

St Albans, or Verulamium, became the third largest town in Roman Britain and a place of considerable importance for almost four centuries, but the 200-acre (80ha) settlement above the River Ver had a rather chequered history. It took its name from an existing tribal settlement of the Catuvellauni, who had moved to the site in about 20 BC from their earlier capital at Wheathampstead. Early on, St Albans was sacked by Boudicca during her spirited revolt (see page 24), when all the buildings were razed to the ground and the inhabitants butchered; a century later it was ravaged by a devastating fire that almost wiped out the town (apparently a layer of ash can still be found below the surface). Despite this, the town was re-established and appeared to prosper, becoming an important market place for local farmers and a centre for trade and shopping. Today's walk takes in a mosaic floor and hypocaust, sections of the town's wall and an open-air theatre, together with a visit to a fascinating and enjoyable museum devoted to the Roman town, giving an excellent impression of what everyday life must have been like around 2,000 years ago.

The walk takes place on the western side of St Albans, and begins at the museum by Verulamium Park, where there's a large car park. Verulamium Museum, which is open daily, was established in 1939, and in 1998 a handsome rotunda and colonnade were added so that the extensive collection is now housed and displayed in a stylish modern environment. Rooms in a wealthy townhouse and a carpenter's workshop have been reconstructed, and there are dazzling

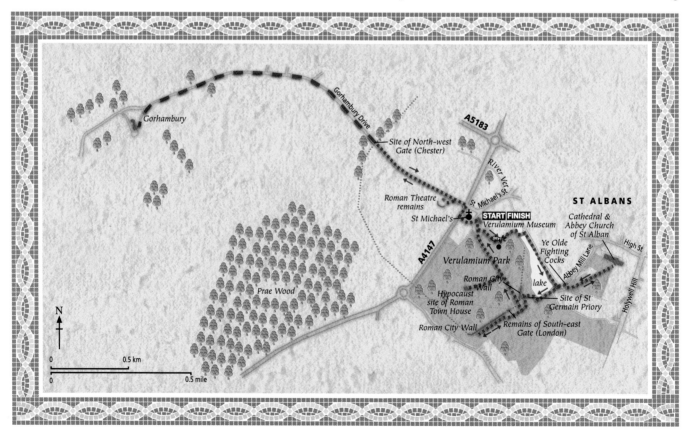

mosaics and wall paintings, and collections of amphorae, coins, jewellery and tools, and coffins complete with skeletons. Above all, the museum examines what went on day by day in this important Roman town – how people lived and what they did for work and entertainment. It also reveals how many of the items such as simple household implements and tools are remarkably similar to what we use today. From pins, buttons and combs through to kitchen knives and work tools, there is much that is familiar to us two millennia later.

With your back to the museum entrance, turn left and follow the surfaced path into the park past the Hertfordshire & Middlesex Wildlife Trust headquarters and garden, then go

ABOVE: The Roman town of Verulamium took its name from the River Ver, and the site was originally a swampy area of meadow and marsh.

ST ALBANS, HERTFORDSHIRE

Start & finish: Verulamium Museum, St Michael's Street, GR 136074
Distance: 3 miles/5km
Time: 2–3 hours
Terrain: Easy surfaced paths, suitable for all ages and abilities
Maps: OS Explorer 182: St Albans & Hatfield; *St Albans Map Guide* (Michael Graham Publications)
Guidebooks: *Roman Verulamium* – booklet guide by St Albans District Council; *Verulamium – the Roman City of St Albans* by Rosalind Nisbett (Tempus Publishing)
Public transport: Verulamium is served by local buses – see free Interlink public transport guide from Tourist Information Centre
Information: Verulamium Museum 01727 751810; St Albans Tourist Information Centre 01727 864511; www.stalbansmuseums.org.uk/verulamium_museum.htm

ABOVE: The town wall ran for over 2 miles (3km) and included projecting bastions on which catapults could be mounted in case of attack.

left at the café and down to the lakes. Cross over the small bridge, turn right, and follow the waterside path to the end. *Verulamium*, from the Celtic Verlamion or Verlamio, meaning 'the settlement above the marsh', was built on the higher ground above the River Ver. Until a canal was built in the 3rd century, the valley remained damp and swampy. The Romans later established a cemetery down here, and in succeeding centuries it became a medieval fishpond. Today it's the preserve of dog-walkers and joggers, and families out for a Sunday stroll feeding the ducks and swans.

At the end turn left to view Ye Olde Fighting Cocks. Admittedly not Roman, this peculiar octagonal building has appeared in the *Guinness Book of Records* as reputedly the oldest public house in Britain. It was originally a pigeon house (*c.* 1400), partly rebuilt two centuries later when it was popular for cockfighting, and it supposedly even accommodated Olive Cromwell for a night. Continue past the pub and across the end of the road for the short path up to St Albans Cathedral.

The Martyrdom of Alban

The magnificent cathedral building was begun in Saxon times, allegedly on the spot where Alban was put to death in AD 209, becoming the first Christian martyr in Britain. Alban lived in *Verulamium* and was almost certainly a Roman citizen (there are suggestions he may have been a Roman officer). This was a time when Christianity was outlawed and persecution was widespread, but Alban took pity on a Christian priest and offered him shelter. He was so impressed with his devotion that Alban converted to the faith, but after the man escaped, the authorities decided to punish Alban instead. It is reported that he was beheaded – a 'privilege' afforded only to Roman citizens. According to later accounts written by monks, all manner of miraculous happenings took place at this time: the waters of the river dried up

to allow the saint to cross, and the executioner's eyes fell out, to describe two. After his martyrdom the site became the focus for pilgrims, and eventually a church (and later a cathedral) was built on the site using stones and tiles from the Romans' former town across the river.

Return down the path and into the park. Walking past the end of the lake, go straight on up the rising path, diverting to the right across the grass to inspect a surviving section of Roman wall. Now protected by railings, it's known as St Germain's Block, and may have once formed part of the long-vanished medieval chapel of St Germain. The town wall wasn't built until AD 275; until then a simple earthwork defence had sufficed. When complete, the wall ran for over 2 miles (3.6km) around the settlement, and consisted of mortared flint with layers of large red bricks or tiles laid flat through the wall to bond the structure together (these are particularly noticeable today). Originally it stood as high as 16 feet (5m), and was as much as 10 feet (3m) thick at its base. What you see now is mostly the core of the wall, since over time it has lost most of its external flint facing. There's another, much tinier fragment of wall back over near the path. Beyond this is the site of the former south-east (London) gate, and extending up the wooded hillside behind is a much longer stretch of Roman wall.

As you will see from the sketch on the information board, the stone gateway must have been an impressive sight. It was one of four similar gates in the wall, and its outline is marked out in stones on the ground, giving you a good idea of the sheer size of the construction. Flanked by two huge towers, which rose high above the wall, there were separate gates for pedestrians and vehicles, and the sight must have been awe-inspiring for first-time visitors.

The wall extends uphill for some way, with a deep ditch to the left, and is quite atmospheric under the dense tree cover. Unfortunately, today's fenced path comes out on a busy road, with no immediate access back into the park, so turn around and walk back

ABOVE: The site of the London gate on the south-east side of St Albans was where the major Roman thoroughfare of Watling Street entered the town; there were separate entrances for pedestrians and vehicles.

down past the site of the former gate to the junction of paths, and turn left towards the museum. Just after the playground turn left again to walk up to a new and rather intriguing, mostly windowless building, sitting isolated amid the parkland and playing fields. It turns out that it encloses the well-preserved mosaic floor and hypocaust from a wing of a Roman townhouse (opening times are identical to those of the museum's). The beautiful mosaic has 16 floral panels; a short trench has been dug into the corner to show the elaborate hypocaust underpinning the floor (believed to date from AD 160–190). Other original mosaics are on show at the main museum, including one of Oceanus, the sea god, with crab or lobster claws attached to his head, and the Lion and Stag mosaic, depicting a lion holding a stag's head in its mouth.

From outside the building you can look down over the park and see where the surviving wall and site of the London gate indicate the southern and eastern perimeter of the Roman town, with the River Ver (and the modern ornamental lake) in the shallow valley below. The cathedral that today dominates the far hillside was built long after the Romans left, of course.

The Basilica and Forum

Return down the path and turn left to reach the museum once more. Just to the left of the main entrance, the outline of part of an original Roman building is shown on a paved area. From a map on the interpretation panel you will see that St John's Church was built right across the heart of the Roman town, where the basilica (the administrative centre) and forum (market square) once stood. This was the nerve centre, as it were, of *Verulamium*. The basilica comprised a huge main hall over 350 feet (106m) long, with a central nave flanked by separate rooms and offices. It was where the town council and law court met, but it was also the centre of religious affairs and almost certainly incorporated a shrine. Trading and business took place in the forum, a courtyard bordered by covered walkways which usually featured shops and stalls, while above were the likes of storerooms. The forum was an important meeting place, where citizens would gather to exchange news and information – the forerunner of our modern squares and piazzas.

The forum was also the main market for the many landowners whose villas dotted the fertile lands surrounding the town. The word *villa* is from the Latin meaning 'farm', and these large estates usually included a whole series of fields, barns and granaries, and were a key source of not just food but also raw materials used by other craftsmen, including hides, fleeces, bones, and so forth.

St Albans was one of the most important provincial towns in Roman Britain, elevated to the status of a *municipium*, so that its inhabitants were accorded rights not far removed from full Roman citizens. (Such a privilege meant that heretical actions like that of Alban's conversion to Christianity would be punished severely.) It also meant that the townspeople

ROMAN FOOD AND DRINK

Verulamium Museum has some excellent examples of amphorae (see picture), large pottery jars used by the Romans to transport and store commodities such as food and drink and, in particular, two items essential to the Roman table that were not produced in Britain: oil and wine. The shape and design of the amphorae varied widely. The largest held up to 22 gallons (100 litres) and typically were used for wine imported from the Mediterranean region – the rough stuff for the troops, and the decent vintages for the officers and statesmen. Olive oil was stored in a more spherical-shaped jar. Another on show at the museum is thin and bright orange in colour, and described as a 'carrot amphora'; it might have been used to hold dates shipped all the way from modern-day Palestine. Another important foodstuff imported in large quantities was *garum* or *liquamen*, a strong and aromatic fish sauce from Spain and Italy. It was made by mashing down oily, fatty fish such as pilchards, sardines and herring, adding salt and herbs, and leaving it to ferment for a week. It was highly popular with the Romans. As the writer Pliny observed: 'Scarcely any other liquid except unguents has come to be more highly valued, bringing fame even to the nations that make it.'

Other produce came from closer to home, including fish and oysters from the coast of southern England. Cereals and vegetables were grown locally. Bread was a staple, eaten for breakfast and seasoned with honey, dates or olives. The main meal was mid-afternoon, and although the diet of the everyday Romano-British family was quite plain, on special occasions the banquets could be lavish. There are records of the well-to-do households sitting down to a variety of meats, including boar, oysters, dormice, thrushes and peacocks, and of course the wine would be flowing. This two- or three-course meal (something else introduced by the Romans) ended in a dessert of fruit or sweetened cakes. Perhaps some things never change, after all?

were able to raise their own local taxes and enjoy considerable freedom when it came to trade and commerce. Despite Boudicca's attack and the fire the following century, the town was rebuilt and seemed to prosper, growing in size with new buildings appearing, such as bathhouses and temples. St Albans flourished right through to the 5th century, but with the Romans having left for good, a new Saxon settlement located across the river surrounding the shrine to St Alban began to take over.

Walk through the churchyard of St Michael's, founded in AD 943 by Abbot Ulsinus and still retaining some internal walls from Saxon times, plus a Norman window at the eastern end of the north aisle. Much restored in the 19th century, the flint finish of the exterior, in particular, is very attractive.

At the far side of the churchyard you emerge on the busy A4147, which thankfully is negotiated by a pedestrian crossing. Along the driveway opposite is the entrance to the Roman theatre (there's a modest admission charge).

On Stage at the Roman Theatre

The theatre was built some time after AD 160, and originally it was more or less circular. Bordering half of the open centre (called the arena or orchestra) were large banks of seating, divided by gangways. On the far end of the opposite half was the relatively small stage, behind which was the dressing room for the actors or participants. Later redevelopment increased the seating and produced a D-shaped design. All this is evident from the careful excavations that first took place in the 1930s, and the resulting floor plan shows the shape and layout of the theatre in precise detail. It was positioned adjacent to Watling Street in the middle of the town, near the forum and basilica. A triumphal arch, one of three in the town, stood across the street next to the theatre, but this monumental feature was purely symbolic and served no practical function.

Like Roman amphitheatres featured elsewhere in this book, such as Caerleon and Chester, the theatre at St Albans originally staged wrestling and mock combat, wild beast performances, dancing and other general entertainment. Ceremonies such as religious festivals were almost certainly held here as well, since the remains of a Roman temple have been unearthed outside the central entrance to the arena. (An impressive 'lamp chimney' found in the theatre temple can be seen at the museum.) In the centre of the arena was a wooden pillar, possibly used for bear-baiting or tying unfortunate human victims before execution.

At some point the stage was extended outwards into the arena by means of wooden planking, and a roof and pillars were added, one of which has been recreated to show its position. By now the focus of the theatre was the stage rather than the arena, and with extra seating the venue could hold up to 3,500 people. In terms of performances, it is likely that plays and poetry readings dominated, along with religious festivals and various games (they were less costly and messy than the traditional blood sports!). Another interesting fact is that the stage curtain – probably first introduced by the Romans and located to the rear of the stage – was lowered rather than raised at the beginning of a performance, then raised at the end.

From the theatre a short path leads to the site of some early Roman shops, simple timber constructions destroyed in Boudicca's raid, with the precise layout of the carpenter's, bronzeworker's and wine shop indicated by stone on the ground. They once faced on to Watling Street; nearby was a 2nd-century townhouse with a small shrine attached.

From the theatre continue along Gorhambury Drive, a private road open to the public on foot or bike. It's a pleasant route amid fields and sporadic woodland on the edge of St Albans, and for some of the way it follows the course of the Romans' Watling Street. After ¼ mile (400km), you come to a narrow strip of woodland that marks the site of the northwest (Chester) gate, and the perimeter wall of the Roman settlement. A small section of wall is just discernible in the trees to the left, but sadly there is no public access to it. Further to the west is a linear mound known as the Fosse, a defensive earthwork and trench begun in the 2nd century as part of a scheme to give greater protection to the town, but evidently unfinished as efforts were switched to reinforcing the main wall instead.

The land hereabouts is part of the Gorhambury Estate, and the drive you are on extends all the way round to the stately house itself. It's an easy and very pleasant walk through the parkland, popular with local people, and there and back takes about an hour. Gorhambury was the 16th-century home of Sir Nicholas Bacon, father of statesman and philosopher Sir Francis, and the grand mansion was rebuilt in 1777 in a contemporary classical style. It includes family portraits stretching back many centuries, as well as period carpets and furniture. The house is open to the public on Thursday afternoons from May to September. The extensive grounds include Prae Wood, shown by excavations to have been once home to local, pre-Roman tribes, as well as the Roman theatre and fragments of wall.

To return to Verulamium Museum at the start of the walk, simply retrace your steps along the driveway to the theatre and park.

ABOVE: The layout of 1st-century shops at St Albans, which were destroyed during Boudicca's fiercesome raid on the city.

OPPOSITE: The Roman theatre at St Albans was used for religious ceremonies, among other things; a small temple has been discovered near its entrance.

COLCHESTER

THE TEMPLE OF CLAUDIUS

Colchester, Camulodunum *to the Romans, can justly claim to be the oldest recorded town in Britain. When Claudius led his troops into the native heartlands in* AD 43, *he headed for this important tribal centre, which had been the capital of the all-powerful King Cunobelin. After some quick military successes and the surrender of local chieftains, probably helped by the no doubt terrifying appearance of Romans riding in on elephants brought over specially for the purpose, the Romans' first permanent settlement in Britain was established at the hilltop site above the River Colne. When most of the Roman troops departed a few years later, Colchester went on to become a thriving civilian town — the Romans' first* colonia, *or highest-ranking settlement in the province. It was officially named* Colonia Claudia, *after the emperor, pre-dating even the founding of London by a handful of years. In this respect, Colchester can claim to be the original capital of Roman Britain.*

The walk begins at Castle Museum, housed in the largest Norman keep in Europe, which is now in a lovely park near the centre of the town. Although missing its upper floors and having been rather battered during the Civil War, what remains of the 11th-century defence is mainly made up of brick and stone from the original Roman settlement. Despite some modern patching up, it's still an imposing edifice, and the perfect place to house the town's rich historical collection. Here you will find a comprehensive display of Roman finds from Colchester and the surrounding area, as well as information,

reminders and relics from other eras of the town's colourful past. It's all presented in a very accessible and family-friendly manner, so that you can try on a toga, or even imprison a willing slave in chains and a metal collar.

There are also guided tours to the vaults below the castle, since the Normans built their stronghold on the base of a Roman temple, and some of the 1st-century foundations are still visible. The Temple of Claudius was begun in AD 54 following the death of the emperor who had spearheaded the invasion of Britain (notwithstanding Julius Caesar's earlier foray). Emperor-worship

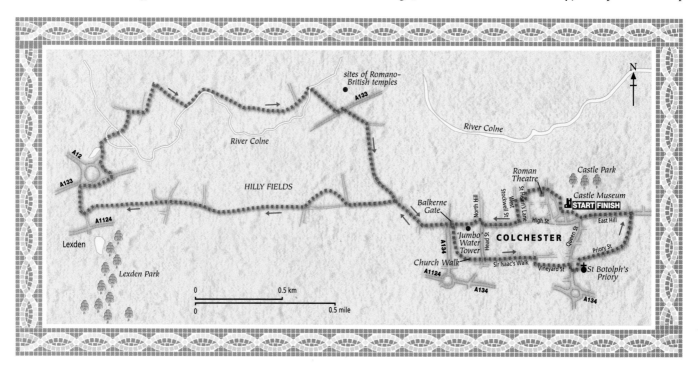

was encouraged by the Romans, who believed it promoted loyalty and obedience, and certainly this gigantic stone temple must have been an impressive monument. It was built along classical lines, with a high podium and rows of ornate columns. However, some time around AD 60 or 61, construction was rudely interrupted by Boudicca and several thousand irate locals. The revolt by the native Icenis, together with the Trinovantes, is described in detail at the museum (and see Peddars Way, pages 20–29), which even features

ABOVE: Colchester Castle, which has the largest Norman keep in Europe, is built on the site of an important Roman temple.

COLCHESTER, ESSEX

Start & finish: Colchester Castle Museum, GR 997249
Distance: 6 miles/9.7km
Time: 4–5 hours
Terrain: Town-centre pavements and unsurfaced paths across fields
Map: OS Explorer 184: Colchester
Guidebooks: *City of Victory: The story of Colchester* by Philip Crummy (Colchester Archaeological Trust); *The Boudiccan Revolt against Rome* by Paul Sealey (Shire Archaeology)
Public transport: Saturday park-and-ride service for town centre (follow signs)
Information: Colchester Tourist Information Centre 01206 282920; Colchester Castle Museum 01206 282939; www.colchestermuseums.org.uk

a life-size replica of Boudicca's chariot designed for a recent TV film about the legendary leader. The uprising was so ferocious that the town was razed to the ground and the entire population of 30,000 – every man, woman and child – was slaughtered. A particular focus for the natives' ire was the half-built temple, a powerful symbol of Roman subjugation. With inadequate defences and the main body of the Roman army far away, the desperate townspeople took refuge in the temple and for two days defied the attackers before being overrun. Subsequent excavations in Colchester have unsurprisingly revealed a thick layer of burnt remains from that time. In fact, a tiny section of authentic Roman wall from the town is on show at the museum, the timbers and wattles almost completely burnt away, leaving just the clay daub.

Despite the setback – and losing your entire population must have been quite a blow – work on the temple resumed some time later, albeit in a modified form. Today, in the vaults below the castle, you can see the foundations of the temple, with imprints of the original wooden shuttering used by the Romans. There's also an oyster shell embedded in the temple wall, an indication that even then the famous Essex seafood was much in demand.

DEATH AND THE AFTERLIFE

In the 1980s, when work to build a new police station began on Butt Road to the south of Colchester town centre, a huge Roman cemetery was discovered. As many as 700 Roman burial plots were unearthed, and two separate cemeteries emerged. The first dated from the 3rd century and its plots were aligned north to south; the other was probably established a century later, and with its graves aligned east to west suggested an association with a nearby Christian church. (If you take a diversion off the main walking route, via the underpass below Southway at the foot of Headgate, you can see the site of this church laid out on the ground.) The Castle Museum has on show a fine collection of Roman coffins from this and other local cemeteries, with one intact lead specimen incorporating a pipe through which mourners poured food and drink for the dead. They also left offerings or so-called grave goods, including pots, various charms and sometimes a coin – to pay the charge levied by Charon, who ferried the dead across the mythical River Styx to the Underworld. Indeed, some of the coffins are decorated with scallop shell designs, reflecting a belief in the journey taken by the dead across the water to the Afterlife. The Romans clearly took death and the Afterlife very seriously. Roman law decreed that the inhabitants of towns must be buried in cemeteries outside the town boundary, and as a result the roads in and out of settlements were lined with large graveyards, such as the one on Butt Road. Burial plots were often marked with elaborately decorated tombstones, some of which still survive. As you enter Castle Museum, look out for the 'Colchester Sphinx', found near the Balkerne Gate in 1821. The small sculpture was probably part of a Roman tomb, and depicts a man's head (almost certainly the deceased) between the paws of the Sphinx – traditionally the symbol of death.

ABOVE: Guided tours take visitors down to the castle vaults, where the foundations of the original Roman temple can still be seen.

ABOVE RIGHT: Chariots of Fire – Boudicca's legendary war wagon, as it may have looked, is on display at the Castle Museum.

RIGHT: The Castle Museum holds many fine mosaics recovered from the Roman town, including the so-called Beryfield pavement.

ABOVE: The Balkerne Gate remains the oldest surviving Roman gateway in Britain, and was once a main entrance to Camulodunum. What can be seen here was one of the two pedestrian passageways which stood beside the vehicular entrance.

Shellfish, and oysters in particular, were popular with the Romans, so that Roman Colchester had its own fishing fleet based at Hythe on the estuary of the River Colne. The tradition continues to this day, with an annual Colchester Oyster Festival.

From Theatre to Chapel

Facing the main entrance to Castle Museum, go round to the left of the castle on the path through the park. Behind the building is a broad, tree-lined rampart – at the foot of this, leave the park via a small gate on the left and, cutting between houses, emerge on Maidenburgh Street. On the opposite corner is St Helen's Chapel, generally believed to be Norman in origin, but according to some experts possibly dating from as early as the 8th century. Today a Greek Orthodox church, it's named after the town's patron saint and first wife to Emperor Constantius Chlorus, who, according to legend, originally built the chapel for her prayers. Tradition also has it that her son was born here, and he, of course, was Constantine the Great, the first Christian ruler of the Roman Empire, and who was proclaimed Emperor while staying in York (see pages 78–87). The chapel was built on the site of a Roman theatre, and if you go up the street a few paces you will see a curving band of darker bricks set out in the road surface. This marks the outer wall of the auditorium, and through a glass window in a building on the right you can see a few excavated remains and a large and colourful mural of what the theatre might have looked like in its heyday.

Go back down to the chapel and turn left into St Helen's Lane. This is known as the Dutch Quarter. As many as 1,600 Flemish refugees settled in the town towards the end of

the 1500s and helped set up a thriving textile industry here. At the corner at the far end, go left then right to walk down Quakers Alley. At the end turn left, up West Stockwell Street past St Martin's Church, which incorporates recycled Roman bricks in its tower. Turn right along the High Street, go over the pedestrian crossing at the very far end and walk along Balkerne Passage located virtually opposite. Continue past the massive brick water tower, built in 1882 and known locally as 'Jumbo', behind which is the Mercury Theatre, named after the Roman god of travellers and merchants.

Beyond the theatre is the Balkerne Gate, the oldest surviving Roman gateway in Britain. There were possibly up to six gateways in the town's walls, but the Balkerne Gate was the main entrance to Roman Colchester. There were once four separate gates here – two smaller side passages for pedestrians and larger central ones for traffic. Just two arches and what was probably the guards' room remain standing today, for originally the structure would have spread across the site occupied by the modern pub nearby. In fact, the Balkerne Gate pre-dates the actual wall, since it was believed to have been built originally as a triumphal arch following the initial Roman conquest, and only later was it incorporated into the new wall. The town itself, once it had recovered from Boudicca's attack, developed into a large and thriving civilian centre, possibly housing as many as 10,000 people (a figure not achieved by modern Colchester until the late 18th century). According to Tacitus, it was 'a strong *colonia* of ex-soldiers established on conquered territory, to provide protection against rebels and a centre for instructing the provincials in the procedures of law'. It had the usual shops and services of any well-developed Roman town, and as we have

ABOVE: The Balkerne Gate and a surviving stretch of wall, with the appropriately named Hole in the Wall pub beyond.

already seen that included a theatre and grand temple. In fact, there were numerous temples in and around the town, plus a second theatre sited on the edge of the town at Gosbecks. It is thought that this larger auditorium, built near the site of the native Britons' original settlement, might have held up to 5,000 people, making it one of the largest Roman theatres of its kind found in Britain.

There was almost certainly a mosaicists' workshop in Colchester, as there was in most large Roman towns. You can see some of their handiwork in the museum, including the Middleborough Mosaic laid in AD 175 in a wealthy town house just outside Colchester, whose central panel depicts two cupids wrestling. During the 2nd century, Colchester was also home to a flourishing pottery industry, in particular supplying the Roman army with earthenware. Everything from coarse pots and dishes through to fine ware for special occasions was produced here; it is the only place in Roman Britain known for certain to have produced the distinctive Samian Roman pottery (usually imported from Gaul). Together with other evidence of large-scale manufacturing in and around the town, it was testimony to Colchester's ongoing wealth and status.

Another feature of Roman Colchester, sadly long disappeared, was a stone-built circus where chariot racing took place. It was 350 yards (350m) long, or the size of three football pitches end to end. Between four and twelve chariots, pulled by as many as ten horses each, raced each other round the track at speeds of up to 45mph (75kph). It must have been quite a spectacle, to say the least.

Hilly Fields and the Colne Valley

From the Balkerne Gate, by the appropriately named Hole in the Wall pub, the walk heads out to Hilly Fields and the Colne valley and a lovely rural interlude, but if you are pressed

BELOW: Picturesque meadows edge the River Colne, and were the site of several Romano-British temples.

for time this could be omitted to create a much shorter and exclusively pavement walk.

Go over the footbridge above the A134 dual carriageway, pausing on the far side to look back and admire how the Roman wall extends down the hill beside the road in both directions. Walk along Popes Lane, opposite, and at the end go over the road by the entrance to the new housing development for the public footpath downhill. In the trees at the bottom of the slope, take the fork half-left (signposted 'Lexden' – you will return on the one ahead via Sheepen Lane) and walk out onto Hilly Fields. Take the left of the paths and proceed up the gentle slope until you reach the open hilltop with the purpose-laid 'easy access' circuit.

Hilly Fields is a local nature reserve managed by Colchester Borough Council, and a wonderful vantage point over the River Colne to the west of the town (in geological terms it is actually a raised river beach formed thousands of years ago by changing sea levels). When you reach the semi-surfaced trail go right and follow it in an anti-clockwise direction around the edge of the

hilltop, looking down over the mix of scrub, woodland, heath and grassland. There are several interpretation boards, telling you among other things that Hilly Fields was once an industrial centre where pre-Roman kings minted coins; a Roman armoury and brick kilns have also been identified on the site.

At the far end of the looping path, by the barrier to a residential road, go right and resume the public right of way along the edge of the reserve. Continue on this obvious route and, approaching the houses of Lexden, pass Buntings Meadow butterfly trail on your right. The path emerges on Elianore Road; walk this to the far end and cross over Glen Avenue. Take the signposted public footpath parallel with Bramley Close, following it through Lexden Springs nature reserve to the lane at the far end. Go right, past the Old Rectory care centre, and then veer right at the busy roundabout to cross the main road via the pavement and pedestrian islands. Continue anti-clockwise to the next exit (Spring Lane) and walk along this much quieter thoroughfare for about ¼ mile (400m), turning off right at the bend on Bakers Lane where there's a sign for Cymbeline Meadows farm trail.

Cymbeline Meadows is an area of working farmland owned by the town council and managed as a recreational facility. Go along the gated lane past the tennis courts as far as a small car park, then turn right on the wheelchair-friendly path indicated 'Sheepen Road'. This lovely route through the meadows beside the meandering River Colne is rich in

ABOVE: The 2nd-century Middleborough mosaic, on show at the Castle Museum, came from a wealthy town house to the north of Colchester.

This original Roman drain arch allowed the town's waste water to empty into a ditch beyond the town walls.

OPPOSITE, BELOW: The Roman wall adjoining Priory Street was severely damaged during a Civil War siege in 1648, and required some major repair work.

BELOW: The 12th-century St Botolphs priory was partly built from plundered Roman stone.

wildlife – dragonflies, birds, butterflies – and picnic tables and benches make a refreshment stop very tempting. Beyond a kissing gate the route underfoot turns from semi-surfaced track to grassy meadow; at the far end go right over a footbridge to reach the main road once more. (Near here, by the way, is the site of several Romano-British temples, although there's nothing to be seen today.) Cross with care via the pedestrian island, then on the far side walk up Sheepen Road for 200 yards. Take the public footpath on the right, opposite the school, and follow this (or more preferably the edge of Hilly Fields above and to your right) back to Popes Lane and the footbridge to Balkerne Gate.

Defending the Town

Facing Balkerne Gate from the footbridge, turn right and walk along the pavement beside the Roman wall. Go up the steps on the left and through a gap in the wall to reach St Mary's Church. Follow the path through the churchyard to the right of the building and out along the street at the end (Church Walk). Cross over Head Street and walk along Sir Isaac's Walk opposite. The modern shopping centre on the left was built on the site of the original legionary fortress, since the 20th Legion and two auxiliary units were initially stationed here when the Romans established the original settlement in AD 43. Six years later most of the troops departed as the legion moved to its new base at Chester (see pages 68–77), leaving mainly retired legionaries and a growing civilian population behind. The 20th Legion went on to play a central role in quelling Boudicca's revolt, gaining its 'Valeria Victrix' moniker in the process, but of course it came too late to help Colchester's largely defenceless inhabitants.

Turn right, down Vineyard Steps, and out (left) across the car park below. Looking back, you can clearly see how the Roman wall underpins the modern shops and buildings. The wall has inevitably been repaired and strengthened since cottages that once backed on

to the Roman defence were removed in the 1960s. Over to the right is a large, arched Roman drain that was included in the actual fortifications.

The town's first walls were built after Boudicca's attack, probably between AD 65 and 80, and were on average 8 feet 8 inches (2.6m) thick. They incorporated a rubble and mortar core, and were faced with layers of brick and, in the absence of any decent local building stone, a hard clay stone known as septaria. The walls were originally free standing, but an earth rampart was later added to the inside. They were about 12 feet (3.6m) high; with a parapet they came to about 18 feet (5.6m).

Walk along Vineyard Street and at the end go right into St Botolph's Street, cross over, and take St Botolph's Church Walk to reach the remains of the 12th-century priory, the first Augustinian religious house in England, which, like other historic buildings around the town, includes Roman bricks and stones in its walls and columns. Follow the path to its left, then turn right to walk along Priory Street. Again, you can see the remains of the Roman wall across to the left on the far side of the car park, but here it's been patched up with newer red brick in a number of places, since it suffered considerable damage during the Civil War when Parliamentary forces besieged the town for eleven weeks in the summer of 1648. Afterwards the victorious General Fairfax ordered that the walls be completely demolished, but fortunately his orders were largely ignored and only the parapets were dismantled.

At the far end of Priory Street turn left and follow East Hill back up to the castle.

CHESTER

A WALK ROUND THE FORTRESS WALLS

The Roman fortress of Deva or Chester was constructed between AD 76 and 80, and provided the third legionary base in the province of Britannia — the others were York and Caerleon. It was established in a loop of the River Dee, hence its name, and although tidal the river could still be crossed at this point. The fortress covered around 61 acres (25ha) and for most of its life was the base for the 20th Valeria Victrix Legion, who were instrumental in consolidating the Romans' control over north Wales and north-west England. But, as we shall see in the story of the amphitheatre, the politics of Rome could be a dangerous and bloody matter, and some of these legionaries may have paid a high price for supporting a rebel commander.

Chester is one of the most impressive walled cities in Britain, and although much of what is visible today is medieval in origin, the foundations are authentically Roman. Indeed, the city is justly proud of its Roman heritage; between June and September, look out for the Roman soldier patrols around the city centre, as young legionaries in full costume lead tours of the amphitheatre

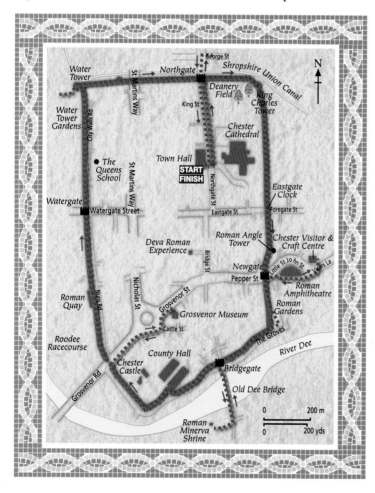

and other remains (check the tourist information centre for full details). This walk follows the walls for their entire length, with various excursions to visit key Roman sites, and although level for long stretches does include some narrow sections and steps.

Begin at the town hall and tourist information centre on Northgate Street in the city centre. With your back to this imposing building, turn left and walk along Northgate Street as far as the city walls, where you should go up the steps onto the elevated walkway. Turn right, and with the Shropshire Union Canal far below to your left, walk along the wall to King Charles Tower on the north-east corner of the original Roman fortress. The small playing field (Deanery Field) below was once the site of the Roman barracks which housed the 5,500 or so troops of the 20th Valeria Victrix ('brave and victorious') Legion, a name it gained following its role in quelling Boudicca's revolt (see page 59).

Continue southwards past the distinctive red sandstone cathedral, founded as a Saxon minster, rebuilt as a Benedictine abbey, then touched up in Victorian times. Beyond this is Eastgate, an imposing 18th-century arch whose famous clocktower was built to celebrate Queen Victoria's Diamond Jubilee in 1897. It was constructed on the site of the *porta principalis sinistra*, one of the four main gates in the Roman fortress. From here roads ran to London and York, while another connected Chester with the city of Wroxeter (near Shrewsbury) on a road known to historians as Welsh Watling Street. This was an extension of the famous Roman road that ran from the Channel ports of Kent via *Londinium* (London) and the Midlands, much of which is familiar to today's motorists as the A5.

CHESTER, CHESHIRE

Start & finish: Town Hall, Northgate Street, GR 405665
Distance: 3 miles/5km
Time: 3 hours
Terrain: Surfaced paths and pavements with steps
Maps: OS Explorer 266: Wirral & Chester; *The All In One Street Map: Chester* (Wordplay)
Guidebooks: *Roman Chester* – booklet by Complete Guides/Chester City Archaeological Service; *Walks around Chester Walls* – leaflet guide from Chester Tourist Information Centre
Public transport: Park-and-ride bus services run from locations around the city
Information: Chester Tourist Information Centre 01244 402111; www.chester.gov.uk/tourism_and_leisure.aspx; Grosvenor Museum 01204 402008

BELOW: The Shropshire Union Canal lies far below Chester's historic city walls.

Continue along the wall, a popular and high-level route sandwiched between the more modern buildings. Chester's historic walls, established by the Romans as simple turf barriers and later rebuilt in stone, completely encompass the city centre. They were strengthened and fortified in the Middle Ages, then rebuilt after damage during the Civil War, and today provide a wonderful and virtually continuous tour of old Chester. There are information panels at various locations, and with plenty of cafés and pubs along the route and the central area only ever a few minutes' walk away, it makes for a delightful walk.

Approaching Newgate, look down on your immediate left for the foundations of the Romans' Angle Tower, marking the south-eastern edge of the fortress, while across the road you will have your first view of the famous amphitheatre. Go over the restored medieval gate, then take the steps down to the road and head for the amphitheatre.

The Amphitheatre's Secrets

The Roman amphitheatre is the largest of its kind found in Britain, but was only discovered as recently as 1929 when work on an underground boiler room for the building next door revealed a curious curved stone wall. At one point Chester Corporation was going to build a new road through the middle of the site, but fortunately common sense prevailed and Little St John Street now bends around the antiquity. Since excavations began in 1960, only the northern half of the arena has been opened up, and the latest dig has been

ABOVE: The foundations of the Romans' south-east angle tower represent one corner of Chester's original Roman fortress.

LEFT: Excavations are ongoing at Chester's Roman amphitheatre, which was 'discovered' just 75 years ago

A DAY OUT AT THE AMPHITHEATRE

When full, Chester's amphitheatre held around 8,000 spectators, with tiers of seats banked high above the central arena. The men occupied the front, while the women and slaves were forced to sit high up at the back.

The word 'arena' comes from the Latin *harena*, meaning sand, with which the ground was covered. It not only provided a soft surface, but also soaked up blood, with slaves sprinkling fresh sand after each bout. The day's events usually began in the morning with so-called beast hunts, involving the baiting of animals such as bulls and bears, and the ritual slaughter of other creatures in a mock depiction of hunting scenes. Executions of convicted criminals and the like would sometimes come next, followed by gladiatorial contests in the afternoon. Although there was certainly blood-shed, with men (on foot and on horseback) pitched against wild animals as well as each other, contrary to popular belief the gladiators rarely fought to the death. They might have done so in the Colosseum at Rome, but in outlying provinces it was too expensive and wasteful in terms of manpower and equipment. Instead, the fights were probably more like modern wrestling bouts staged for TV, when the spectacle is of more importance than the physical contest.

The amphitheatre was also used for ceremonial parades and military drills, since the legionaries were constantly being put through their paces and had to train daily. Visiting dignitaries would sit in the VIP box with the commanding officers of the legion and review the soldiers and perhaps demon-strations of the latest weapons. Above all, though, the amphitheatre was about showy displays and all-round entertainment designed to engage the population. Local leaders could sponsor specific activities in the arena and garner support and prestige. As the Roman writer Fronto (AD 100–166) wrote: 'The success of the Government depends on amusements as much as serious things… the shows keep the population happy.'

ABOVE: The officers' box at the amphitheatre was reserved for dignitaries.

ABOVE, RIGHT: Off-duty legionaries posing at the optio's mess in the Grosvenor Museum.

trying to discover the origin and purpose of an earlier wooden Roman building discovered at the entrance of the amphitheatre – for more details go to www.chesteramphitheatre.co.uk.

You can explore the site on foot, including the arena – or, at least, the half that is exposed. There are steps up from the arena, and the remains of an officers' box – the Roman equivalent of the VIP box you see at sporting venues today. The amphitheatre was built around AD 100 and lay just outside the Roman fortress. The outer wall of the arena was believed to be as high as 85 feet (26m), and it seated up to 8,000 spectators. By the middle of the 2nd century it is believed to have fallen into decay and was largely used as a rubbish dump, but by the beginning of the 4th century it had been rebuilt and was once more in use. Why was it brought back to life? A suggestion – and only that – surrounds the rebellion led by Britain's governor Marcus Aurelius Carausius in AD 287, which was known to have been supported by one legion in particular. Was that legion the 20th Legion (Valeria Victrix), stationed in Chester? And after Britain was 'reconquered' in AD 296–7, could Chester's amphitheatre have been deliberately renovated in order to publicly execute the ringleaders and humiliate the participating legionaries?

Across the road from the amphitheatre is the Chester visitor and craft centre, which is free to enter and has a handy café, as well as exhibitions on the likes of Roman military armour and the findings of the recent excavations at the amphitheatre.

Retrace your steps towards Newgate, but before the gateway turn left into the so-called Roman Gardens. This narrow strip of land lies in the shadow of the huge medieval walls, and if you look closely you may notice that the walls have been patched up in several places. This followed a siege during the Civil War, when the Royalist city was besieged by the Parliamentary army, who trained their guns on the Cavaliers' defences. Despite this, the star attraction of the garden are the bases and stumps of Roman columns, most of which were once found in the hall of a Roman bathhouse, and also a reconstructed hypocaust using pillars that once stood in the main bath building of the Roman fortress.

In simple terms, a hypocaust was a system of underfloor heating that worked by heated air being fed through a building from the bottom. The tiled floor was raised on

ABOVE: A shrine to the goddess of wisdom and the arts, Minerva, stands in what was once Chester's main quarry and the source for the Romans' building stone.

LEFT: Bases and stumps from Roman columns line the so-called Roman Gardens near the amphitheatre.

columns, and an underground or outside furnace directed heat through this space, which would then pass up through the floor, drawn up by hollow box tiles that acted as flues or by actual flues set in the walls. In this way a constant draft of warm air would circulate throughout the building. It was an effective system and widely used in Roman bathhouses, where it would create the extreme level of heat necessary for the hot room (*caldarium*). Private buildings, especially villas, also heated their principal rooms in this way, and you can inspect surviving hypocausts on a number of other walks in this book, including Chedworth, St Albans and Bignor.

A Shrine to Minerva

From the hypocaust you can either rejoin the path along the wall by first going through the small gateway opposite and turning left for the ramp, or else descend through the lower garden to the Groves for the popular, tree-lined waterfront where river cruises operate

ABOVE: The Old Dee Bridge is Chester's oldest river crossing and links England and Wales.

throughout the year. With the River Dee on your left, continue along to the next gate, Bridgegate, completely rebuilt after its destruction in the Civil War.

Now leave the wall and head across the seven-arched Old Dee Bridge over the river. This historic crossing was originally made of wood; its stone replacement was built in the 1300s, and for five centuries the Old Dee Bridge remained Chester's only crossing point into Wales. Go over to the far bank and in a few paces turn right into a public garden called Edgar's Field. Here the Romans had their main quarry, from which most of the sandstone used in the construction of Deva came. A small part of the old quarry face can still be seen, and carved into the rock is a badly weathered figure. It's believed to be of Minerva, the Roman goddess of warriors and craftsmen, and was perhaps a Roman quarrymen's shrine (a cast of the shrine can be found at the city's Grosvenor Museum). Minerva is identifiable — but only just, it must be said — by her traditional symbols of an owl and warlike clothing, including a helmet, shield and spear. The fact that the shrine has survived for so long and escaped the attentions of vandals may be because for many years it was mistaken as a carving of the Virgin Mary.

Re-cross the bridge and turn left, and on the far side of county hall the city wall resumes. As it swings around to the north-west, following the river, it affords good views of Chester Castle, originally built as a motte and bailey by William the Conqueror in 1077, then later a more permanent stone affair. After becoming dilapidated it was remodelled in 1788–1822 by Thomas Harrison in a neoclassical style. Incidentally, the same architect was responsible for designing Grosvenor Bridge across the river to your left, which when it was opened in 1832 was the largest single-span stone bridge in the world.

When you reach Grosvenor Road, turn right and head towards the city centre on a brief

detour. Go over the roundabout in front of the castle and crown court to visit Grosvenor Museum. This splendid civic museum (open daily and free to enter) gives a fascinating insight into life in Roman Chester, including a reconstruction of an optio's office — he was the garrison's clerk and bookkeeper, second-in-command to the centurion. The museum also houses the largest collection of tombstones and monuments from a single Roman site in Britain, many of which were subsequently used to repair the city walls and only redis-covered at the end of the 1800s. There's also information on the Romans' attempts to mine lead from the Halkyn mountain area to the south-east near Wrexham, plus some rather unusual features, including examples of genuine Roman luggage labels, made from metal and used for items in transit. There's also an explanation of how Roman locks worked (apparently they slid and locked) and a brief guide to numeracy Roman-style with the help of a contemporary calculator — an abacus.

Another interesting exhibit is an expertly made scale model of the legionary fortress *circa* AD 220, showing not just the barrack blocks and military buildings crammed close together within the walls, but also the location of the quarry and harbour — you will come to the harbour shortly.

From Quayside to Racecourse

Return to the river and go over Grosvenor Road at the pedestrian crossing and on to Nuns Road alongside Chester racecourse. It's known as the Roodee, from the Old English 'rood' (cross) and 'eye' (island) — the stump of a medieval cross is still visible in the middle of the circuit. It is a unique course in more ways than one. First, almost the entire 1 mile 49 yards (1.65km) of the track is curved, save for the short home straight, which is a bit of a blow

ABOVE: Morbidly fascinating — Grosvenor Museum's impressive display of tombstones is the largest from a single Roman site in Britain.

ABOVE: *Chester's Roodee racecourse was once a tidal basin where Roman ships would berth.*

OPPOSITE: *Begun in Roman times and developed throughout the Middle Ages, Chester's city walls are remarkably intact, as can be seen here, at Northgate.*

if you're drawn on the outside or if your horse doesn't cope too well with bends. But more remarkable is that the Roodee was once a vast tidal basin where Roman cargo ships would moor, bringing their cargoes of figs, oil, wine and fish sauce from far-off places. The wall you are standing on was once the embankment, and the lower section is certainly Roman (there is said to be a further 15 feet or 4.5m under the current ground level); unless it's race day, you can go down the steps opposite Black Friars and examine the wall for yourself. Here on the quayside two thousand years ago, wooden jetties would have extended into the water and it would no doubt have been a busy scene. In the centuries after the Romans left, the quayside was used less and less. By the Middle Ages the shallow waters had silted so that the former river was eventually used for grazing, and in 1539 horse racing began.

The city wall continues beyond the racecourse over the pedestrian bridge at Watergate and on past The Queens School to the so-called Watch Tower. This represented the north-west corner of the medieval walls and, like the quayside further back, was beyond the original defences of the Roman fort. However, it's worth visiting for the short detour down the steps to the public gardens below. The centrepiece of the Water Tower Gardens is an intricately constructed maze of different coloured paths, and these converge on a central mosaic of a dolphin that is based on a Roman motif found in Chester.

Carry on along the wall, now heading eastwards above the canal once more, and go over the dual carriageway and on as far as Northgate, where you began your wall walk. Descend the steps and turn left, beneath Northgate, in order to look back at the wall from the canal bridge (or even George Street further on). If you look closely, you can see where the masonry bulges outwards — believed to be remnants of the original Roman wall.

Turn round and walk back along Northgate Street to the start of the walk. Note the Roman column and bases standing beside the pavement just along from the town hall, resurrected in 1981 when Chester won the European Prize for the Preservation of Historic Monuments. There are also several other sites where small sections of Roman Chester are still visible, including sections of hypocaust in the basements of shops at 14 Northgate Row and 39 Bridge Street, and the base of a column from the headquarters building underneath 23 Northgate Street.

If you've visited the Grosvenor Museum and want to learn still more about Roman Chester, then consider a visit to the Dewa Roman Experience on Pierpoint Lane (off Bridge Street). They say it's spelled 'Dewa' because that's how Chester's Roman name *Deva* was pronounced, but either way this privately run visitor attraction has, among other things, an interesting collection of Roman oil lamps, coins, jewellery and weaponry. In particular, there's a 'hands-on' room that is popular with younger visitors, where you are encouraged to design your own mosaic, construct a hypocaust and try on a replica Roman helmet and body armour (there's a mirror in which to admire yourself).

YORK

THE ROMANS' NORTHERN POWER BASE

The lively, bustling city of York has come a long way since AD 71 when the 9th Legion, sent north from Lincoln (Lindum) to quell the feuding Brigantes, decided to set up camp on a sandstone plateau between the rivers Ouse and Foss. Named Eboracum, after a Celtic word meaning the place where the yew tree grows, it became the base for the 9th Legion and the Romans' military operations in northern Britain. Its importance was cemented in AD 208 when Emperor Septimus Severus established the Imperial Court in York and effectively ruled the whole of the Roman Empire from this spot for the next three years. Later, York was made capital of Lower Britain (Britannia Inferior) and with a large civilian settlement surrounding the military garrison it was awarded the status of colonia, allowing it the freedom of self-government. When the 9th Legion left they were replaced by the 6th Victrix, which remained based at York until the Romans all went home in AD 410. But by then York's pre-eminence was well established.

Your first decision in this handsome and history-rich city is whether to look around the Yorkshire Museum prior to your walk or after. I would suggest visiting before you set off, since it will give you an excellent introduction to Roman York and make your tour of the city more rewarding. The museum, which is open daily, is set in leafy grounds close to the city centre on the banks of the River Ouse, and has splendid displays on many different aspects of the county's history, including Roman, Viking and Norman finds. The Roman exhibits include pendants and compasses as well as ballista balls and fragments of armour. A replica slate gaming board comes complete with authentic bone dice and stone counters, and there are other everyday domestic items, such as hairpins, leather footwear, bronze bowls and strainers. There is genuine human hair discovered beneath a Roman coffin, and numerous altars and tombstones, such as that of L. Duccius Ruffinus, a 28-year-old standard-bearer from Gaul, found in the city at Micklegate. A life-size model of a legionary soldier, with armour, helmet, javelin and dagger, stands guard near the entrance. Note his traditional sandals, introduced to Britain by the Romans and mostly worn by the legionaries.

Allow yourself plenty of time to do the museum justice, and remember that the museum is not just famous for its indoor exhibits. In the 10-acre gardens are the remains of the Benedictine St Mary's Abbey, and the restored, 14th-century Hospitium, thought to have been built as a guest house for visitors to the abbey. But closer still to the main building – just a few yards to the east – is the so-called Multangular Tower. This huge, ten-sided stone construction marks the western corner of the original Roman fortress, and although it was subsequently

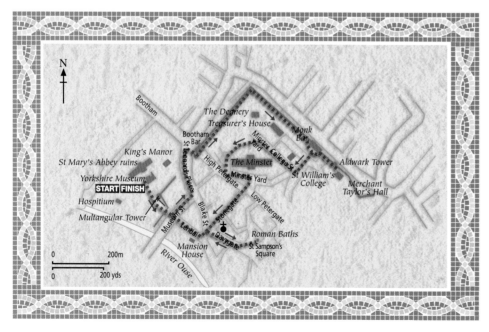

built upon during the Middle Ages, the original Roman defence is evident in the smaller stones and band of red tiles towards the bottom. On either side of the 20-foot-high (5.8m) tower are surviving sections of the original Roman wall, and if you go through the small gateway in the wall to the side of the tower you can also see several Roman coffins. From here a path runs alongside the wall to the so-called Anglian Tower, built in the 7th century in a breach of the Roman wall. Beyond here are markers in the high bank showing the different layers of the city's early history – from its founding by the Romans through the Dark Ages to the Norman Conquest and medieval period.

ABOVE: The huge Multangular Tower represented the western corner of the legionary fortress and, despite medieval additions, its lower section is palpably Roman.

YORK, NORTH YORKSHIRE

Start & finish: Yorkshire Museum, GR 598522
Distance: 2 miles/3.2km
Time: 2–3 hours
Terrain: Surfaced paths and pavements, but steep steps down from the city wall
Maps: OS Explorer 290: York; *York City Atlas* (Collins)
Guidebooks: *Roman York from AD 71* by Herman Ramm (York Archaeological Society); *Roman York* – leaflet guide from York Tourist Information Centre
Public transport: Park-and-ride bus services run every 10 minutes or so from locations around the city
Information: York Tourist Information Centre 01904 550099; www.visityork.org; Yorkshire Museum 01904 687687; www.yorkshiremuseum.org.uk; www.yorkromanfestival.co.uk

ABOVE: Roman coffins can be found in and around the gardens of the Yorkshire Museum; most are believed to be empty!

From the museum and tower, follow the wide path to the main gate and turn left onto Museum Street. With the bridge over the river behind you, head up towards the minster and then left on to St Leonard's Place. Note the tiny surviving stretch of 4th-century Roman wall, preserved by the car park of the council offices opposite the theatre. Only the top part is visible – excavations have shown that another 11 feet (3.3m) of Roman wall lie buried below. Beyond is King's Manor, the striking 13th-century former abbot's residence, and almost next to it the more modern but no less imposing city art gallery. Here go over the road by the pedestrian crossing to reach Bootham Bar, one of York's four medieval city gates. However, it was also the north-western gateway into the Roman fortress, and the road opposite (Bootham) still heads with typical straightness out of the city. As the military headquarters for the Romans in northern England, this thoroughfare would have seen regular troop movements as the legionaries were sent out to quell unrest or reinforce defences on Hadrian's Wall, which was known to have been overrun and even abandoned for a while.

Keeping Guard on the Wall

Unless you want to go into the tourist information centre (virtually next door), go up the steps of the mighty gatehouse and through the building to step out onto the city wall. The well-preserved, high-level walkway provides an excellent pedestrian route around the inner, northern part of historic York. There are wonderful views across to the minster on your right, with the peaceful grounds of the minster library and deanery in the foreground. York's historic city walls are among the most intact of any British town or city. As we've already seen at the museum gardens, the origin or foundation of the walls along this stretch is indeed Roman, and the route you are following is without doubt the north-east and north-western defensive perimeter of the original Roman fortress. However, most of the stone defence visible today dates from the early medieval period (with some minor patching up by the Victorians), and this later walled city is significantly larger than the original Roman fort – 260 acres (105ha) against the Romans' 50-acre (20-ha) walled site. The Romans' garrison in fact occupies just the northern corner of the medieval city, so that most of the surviving and much-photographed city walls date from the 13th century.

Continue as far as Monk Bar, another preserved gatehouse dating from the 14th century, where you have to descend a steep and narrow interior staircase to the pavement below. Incidentally, as well as including a working portcullis, the first-floor guard room of the gatehouse houses the Richard III Museum (open daily), dedicated to clearing the name of this much-maligned English king.

Go across the road and, trying to avoid the temptations of the Monk Bar Chocolatiers, ascend the steps to regain the wall and resume your progress along the battlements. Looking down to your right, into the city, you will notice the remains of what was the eastern corner of the Romans' fortress; unlike the Multangular Tower, all that is left here are three low corner walls. Known as the Aldwark Tower, it represents the site of York's first archaeological excavation in the 1920s. The impressive medieval building just beyond is the Merchant Taylors Hall.

The Ghostly Army

Retrace your steps to Monk's Bar and back down to the pavement and turn left. With the gatehouse behind you, walk along Goodramgate (past Caesar's Pizzeria, towards the city centre) and turn right into College Street, underneath the dramatic overhanging Tudor frontage of the historic corner building. Go past St William's College to Minster Yard and its junction with Chapter House Street. If you turn right down this quiet and inviting cobbled thoroughfare, you come to the entrance of the Treasurer's House, now owned by the National Trust and open to the public. A Roman street called *via decumana* once ran near here, and remarkably it now forms the actual floor of the cellar of the Treasurer's House. In 1953, a local man, Harry Martindale, was at work down there when he heard the sound

ABOVE: The medieval gatehouse at Monk Bar on the north-eastern side of the Romans' original stronghold.

WHATEVER HAPPENED TO THE 9TH LEGION?

The 9th Legion, or IX Hispana (the so-called 'Spanish Legion' after previous campaigns), is famous for founding York, but its uncertain fate has puzzled historians and fuelled much debate. The last we hear of them at York is when they began rebuilding the fort in stone in AD 108. Around AD 120 Emperor Hadrian sent the 9th Legion north to deal with some troublesome natives – and that is the last firm record of them we have. All sorts of explanations and theories have been put forward to account for the 9th Legion's disappearance. It's been suggested that they were one of three legions sent to reinforce Hadrian's Wall, but that they were sent to the turf wall in the west and so left no customary inscriptions in the stones to record their stretch of duty. Another suggestion is that they were completely wiped out in a ferocious battle with the barbarian hordes in Caledonia (Scotland), after which the Romans gave up the dangerous far north and fell back to the new defensive wall. But losing 5,000 men in one go and without any trace seems unlikely. To explain this, one school of thought says that perhaps the Roman soldiers acted with such disgrace that the legion was disbanded and all future mention of it was forbidden. Certainly, Roman historians usually said very little about the legions that were utterly defeated or humiliated in battle. However, most historians now appear to agree that the legion was probably sent back to mainland Europe, and there is an undated record of their presence at Nijmegen (in present-day Netherlands) and later in Germany and locations further east. But the references are hazy and imprecise, and it looks likely that the true fate of this legendary legion will never be known.

of a trumpet. He looked up to see a line of Roman soldiers march straight out of the wall and on past him – visible only from the knees upwards. Later excavations showed that the road had built up over time and the original Roman road was indeed much lower than the present-day one. The small 'ghost cellar' is open to visitors.

Unless you're visiting the Treasurer's House, continue along Minster Yard, through the gate in the black railings (public pedestrian access is allowed), and then cross over for the popular path across the lawns at the foot of the minster. At the magnificent western end of the building, continue all the way round to the main entrance at the south door.

For all its medieval magnificence, what is not immediately obvious about York Minster is that it was built more or less on the site of the legionary's military headquarters, the *principia*, in the centre of the Roman fortress and very much at the heart of York. Following work to strengthen the foundations of the minster in the 1960s – when it was revealed that the entire structure was in danger of crashing down – remains of the earlier Roman occupation were revealed. Painstaking excavations followed, and slowly the layout of the *principia* was pieced together. Various finds are now displayed in the Undercroft Museum beneath the cathedral. These include fragments of painted plaster that have been put back together, as well as objects such as a Roman candlestick, beakers, a bronze key and building tiles. There's even an original Roman culvert (1st–2nd century), which still drains water away and into the River Ouse.

OPPOSITE: York Minster was built on the site of the Romans' headquarters, as excavations into its foundations now testify.

LEFT: A stretch of the York City wall between Monk Bar and Aldwark Tower.

ABOVE: Resurrected outside the minster, this impressive column once supported the city's Roman basilica.

OPPOSITE: Now thronged with shoppers and tourists, Stonegate was one of the two main thoroughfares in Roman York.

Access is from inside the minster, and there is a modest admission charge.

Constantine the Great

Also on display downstairs is an oversized carved head of Emperor Constantine, found in nearby Stonegate. Another, more modern depiction can be found outside the minster, where a superb bronze statue sees Constantine the Great reclining imperiously as he gazes at the throngs of visitors to the minster. This famous and gifted young general was proclaimed Emperor in York by his troops on the death of his father, Constantius Chlorus, in AD 306 – although it took another few years for Constantine to see off five rival claimants for the title. Despite his military prowess, he is particularly remembered for encouraging religious tolerance, permitting Christianity to become a state religion and becoming the first Roman emperor to adopt the Christian faith (although he was baptized only shortly before his death). He chose the Greek city of Byzantium from which to rule his empire, changing its name to Constantinople. Today it is known as Istanbul.

Across the street from the statue is a 31-foot-high (9.5m) Roman column unearthed in the excavations deep below the minster 40 years ago, and one of 16 that originally supported the roof of the great hall (the *basilica*). It was officially erected – for the second time, as it were – in 1971, to commemorate the 1900th anniversary of the founding of York by the Romans. The column is floodlit at night, and according to some experts has been positioned upside down.

With your back to the minster entrance, turn into Minster Gates to reach the junction of Stonegate (*via praetoria*) and Petergate (*via principalis*). These were the two most important streets in the Roman stronghold, leading to the main gates in the wall. The original fortress was small and rectangular, its ramparts made from earth and clay topped with turf, and there were wooden towers at the gateways and timber-framed buildings inside. In AD 107/8 the defences were rebuilt in stone, with exterior walls 6 feet (1.8m) thick, partly as a result of collapse, but also because the fort had been attacked on several occasions. The layout was later redesigned to incorporate six interval towers and two huge angle towers – of which the Multangular Tower is a surviving example – reflecting York's elevated status as the Romans' military capital.

York's pre-eminence is reflected in the fact that the two Roman emperors who died in Britain – Chlorus and Severus – both did so at York. There is no doubt that York must have had palaces and temples in addition to the military garrison, but the civil town that grew up on the south bank of the Ouse was also considerable, and upon becoming a *colonia* even had walls of its own. It included a thriving commercial centre, with boats full of goods and supplies – from wine and olive oil to coal and pottery – sailing up the Foss and Ouse to unload, and all manner of traders and artisans must have been busy supplying the large garrison. Of course, the town also included private residences and

ABOVE: The sarcophagus of Julia Fortunata, who was the wife of a senior Roman official based at York (on display at the Yorkshire Museum).

ABOVE RIGHT: The low walled remains are all that is left of the eastern corner of the Roman's fortress, called the Aldwark Tower.

family dwellings, and we can tell something of this from the Roman burial sites discovered around the city. At the Yorkshire Museum there are several memorial stones and coffins, including the sarcophagus of a woman called Julia Fortunata, from Sardinia. According to the Latin inscription on the side of her tomb, she was a 'loyal wife' to her husband, Verecundius Diogenes, who was a *servir augustalis*, an official responsible for emperor-worship in the *colonia* of York. The museum also has on show a number of Roman lead urns, used in cremations, whose lids have holes in the middle through which a pipe connected them to the surface for libations to be poured on to the remains of the bones. This common Roman ritual was practised in Italy and brought to this country by the legionaries.

Proceed straight on along Stonegate, a paved and pleasantly traffic-free route that is usually busy with shoppers and tourists. At the far end turn left by St Helen's Church until you reach St Sampson's Square. To the left, in the northern corner, is the Roman Baths pub, below which are the remains of a Roman bathhouse (there's an admission fee, and the entrance is through the doorway beside the pub). It's one of the best preserved of its kind in the country, and here you can learn all about an aspect of everyday life that Romans took very seriously. Bath-time for the Romans had a recreational and social function, and the actual process of bathing – the progression from the warm room to the hot, the scraping of the skin, the cold plunge and the massage – was taken very seriously. For more details on this fascinating aspect of everyday Roman life, see page 95.

Retrace your steps to the junction with Petergate on St Helen's Square (with the famous Betty's Tea Rooms on the corner). Go left across the square towards the elegant 18th-century Mansion House, residence of the lord mayor. This was roughly the site of the main gate (*porta praetoria*), double-arched and built to impress, the principal entrance to the Roman city – although nothing remains of it today.

Facing the Mansion House turn right into Lendal, past the post office, and at the far end you emerge on to Museum Street, with the Yorkshire Museum opposite.

York's Roman Festival

If you really want to experience the ultimate in Roman York, then time your visit for a weekend in early August when the city holds its annual Roman Festival. This lively and entertaining event features all manner of activities, including the crowning of Emperor Constantine and a march around the city by several hundred people dressed in Roman costume. There are talks and children's activities, music and dance, wrestling and chariot races, and even a gladiator competition. For full details go to the website listed in the information panel, or call the tourist information centre.

ABOVE: The remains of the Benedictine abbey of St Mary stand in the Museum Gardens beside the River Ouse.

ROMAN BUILDINGS

Despite the growth of towns in Roman Britain, most of the population still lived in scattered farmsteads. However, the new feature in the rural landscape was the villa, a private dwelling usually belonging to a well-to-do Roman or Romano-British family. Some, like Chedworth, gave the impression of a semi-religious community or simply a comfortable retreat in the country, while others (such as Bignor) were major farming concerns owned and managed by a person of considerable social standing. Whatever their exact purpose, these new villas incorporated a number of distinctive Roman features: verandas, walled courtyards and gardens, while inside intricate mosaics decorated the heated floor and elaborate baths and grand living rooms gave the villa an air of opulence. This was clearly the des' res' in Roman Britain.

OPPOSITE: The piscina (water basin) at Bignor Roman Villa is surrounded by an intricate network of mosaics.

CHEDWORTH

A ROMAN IDYLL IN THE COTSWOLDS

Chedworth Roman villa, owned by the National Trust and open to the public throughout the year, is believed to be one of 50 such villas that once dotted the rolling Cotswold Hills. It's located about 8 miles (13km) north of the important Roman town of Corinium *(which we know today as Cirencester), and just off the well-used Roman road called the Fosse Way (the A429 on modern road atlases). All this goes to show that getting on for 2,000 years ago this area must have been busy and to a large extent quite prosperous, with farming estates supplying the traders and market at Cirencester. Plenty of people might have lived in poverty and suffered the daily grind, but for some in Romano-Britain life was comfortable and — for a while, at least — the riches flowed.*

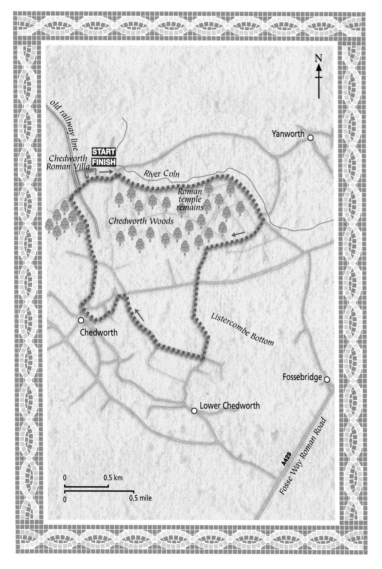

There is limited parking near the entrance of the villa, but you can otherwise use the woodland car park at the beginning of the drive (open April–September, for cars only). The lovely setting at the foot of wooded hillside above the gentle River Coln lends itself to a long and leisurely exploration, and if you want to extend the walk there are possibilities down the valley towards Fossebridge and Lower Chedworth, and other paths through Chedworth Woods.

Walk down the approach drive from the villa and at the road junction at the bottom (not the woodland car park turning just before), go right onto a private drive. A sign confirms that walkers are allowed to use the route since it's a public footpath, so proceed along the firm and wide track along the bottom of the valley. It really is a very pleasant stretch, with the river meadows flanking the meandering Coln spread out to your left. Like many of the clear and delectable Cotswold streams and rivers that run over the limestone, the Coln offers good trout fishing, and at one point the infant river runs alongside the track. On the other side, among the luxuriant, mixed woodland, is the site of a former Roman temple.

After about a mile you pass through a gate and arrive at the bend of a road. Go ahead for a few yards, past the house, and take the waymarked footpath up into the woods to the right. Continue through the trees on a clear path, soon joined by one from the left, and 50m after this veer left and down to the bottom of the shallow but quite open wooded valley (there are wooden posts with

CHEDWORTH, GLOUCESTERSHIRE

Start & finish: Chedworth Roman Villa, GR 054135
Distance: 5 miles/8km
Time: 3–4 hours
Terrain: Variety of woodland field paths, some a little steep, with plenty of stiles
Map: OS Outdoor Leisure 45: The Cotswolds
Guidebook: *Chedworth Roman Villa* by Roger Goodburn (National Trust)
Public transport: Cotswold Lion bus service from Cirencester (summer only)
Information: Cirencester Tourist Information Centre 01285 654180; Chedworth Roman Villa 01242 890256; Corinium Museum 01285 655611

ABOVE: The leafy villa at Chedworth was one of nine in a 5-mile (8-km) radius in the Cotswolds.

waymarks confirming the route). Here turn right and follow the wide grassy track along the valley floor gently uphill, keeping an eye open for the shy fallow deer that roam the ancient woods. The woodland is known as 'ancient' because it was established prior to 1600, and as a result is richer in wildlife and contains more plant species than many newer woods. It might have looked quite similar to the Romans, in fact, save for the more orderly appearance today, and of course the regimented coniferous plantations.

Emerging from the woods, go up to the marker post at the top of the slope and continue southwards across the wide field to the lane on the far side. Crossing the road, pause to admire the exquisite dry-stone walls that you're clambering across, and how the

limestone blocks and slabs have been so expertly knitted together. If you're exploring other walks in this book, compare it to the equally skilful slate walls of the Lake District, for instance, near Hardknott Roman fort.

On the far side of the lane go down through another field and across Listercombe Bottom, then up through the copse on the far side. The path now slants left across the corner of another field and along between a narrow walled strip. At the far end of this you come to a junction with a well-used bridleway. Go right and follow this wide track along the northern rim of the valley, with the buildings of Chedworth glimpsed below. When you eventually meet a surfaced road, go left. At the first corner take the gated path on the left, and at the lower gate drop down across a field and, via a kissing gate, go over a lane for a narrow path down to the stream. Once over the rough slab bridge, continue across the field on the far bank, and beyond the woodland belt (disguising the former railway line) turn right after the stile. On the far side of the field you will pass riding stables to emerge by the Seven Tuns pub.

ABOVE: Chedworth Woods are rich in wildlife, and home to the shy and elusive fallow deer.

OPPOSITE: The villa at Chedworth was sited on a spring and close to the River Coln, since a good water supply was all-important.

Chugging through Chedworth

The former railway line you have just crossed belonged to the Midland and South-western Junction Railway, who opened it in 1891 to connect Swindon to Cheltenham via Cirencester. Its course through the Cotswolds was fraught with difficulties – numerous cuttings, embankments and tunnels were needed, and a tunnel at Chedworth collapsed during construction. The route was used in particular by military personnel, since it passed

ABOVE: Little disturbed over the centuries, the lay-out of the villa at Chedworth is clear and comprehensible, with buildings arranged round a courtyard and along two wings.

Salisbury Plain, but it was never a huge commercial success, and after being taken over by The Great Western Railway the line was eventually closed in 1961. There are old photo-graphs of the line, including Chedworth Station, in the Seven Tuns. This handsome village pub claims to date from 1610 and has two bars full of character. Food and drink is served lunchtime and evening, and there is some particularly attractive outside seating, especially in the terraced garden by the stream across the road.

From the pub take the short path, opposite, past cottages to the Church of St Andrew. Sitting on a higher slope to the rest of the village, the picturesque building contains a Norman tower and a 15th-century 'wine glass' pulpit – but the outside door is often locked.

Continue (northwards) along the lane and at the fork go straight on – there's even a sign for pedestrians to the Roman villa. Go over the stile at the end and left through a long field, aiming for the stile in the wall at the top end. Puff up the steps through a small wood and out along a hilltop path, ignoring paths off the right. From the hilltop there are extensive views over Chedworth Woods and the Coln Valley into the heart of the Cotswolds, but for now your route is back into the trees. Go along the field edge and down the popular path into the woodland. When you come to a four-way junction in a depression, turn right and walk down this bumpy track beneath the former railway bridge to reach the Roman villa.

On the far side of the bridge there are steps up to Gloucestershire Wildlife Trust's nature reserve, which takes the form of a mile-long strip of land – the corridor occupied by the old railway line – through the middle of Chedworth Woods. There's a free leaflet guide to the reserve available from reception at the villa, and among the highlights are roosting bats in the tunnel at the western end, limestone-loving plants such as common

ROMAN BATHING

The bathhouse was an integral feature of everyday Roman life, and whether in a legionary fortress or private villa, such as here at Chedworth, bathing was taken very seriously. There was a precise routine to be followed, depending on the particular layout of the bathhouse, as the bather progressed from room to room. First you would get undressed in the changing room (*apodyterium*) before passing into the warm room (*tepidarium*) to acclimatize. After this came the hot room (*caldarium*), often heated by an underground furnace via a hypocaust, where you were expected to build up a healthy sweat. An attendant would rub oils or perfumes into your skin to help soak up the sweat, then scrape it with a hook-shaped metal implement called a *strigil* to remove all the impurities. There were basins of water to assist bathers in their ablutions, but to cool down after the stifling heat of the hot room (and it could be very hot indeed) you would end with a plunge in

the cold bath (*frigidarium*) before returning to collect your clothes via the warm room. There were many variations on this bathing sequence, and the villa at Chedworth was particularly notable for having both damp-heat and dry-heat bathing suites.

Bathing was very much a communal activity, and apart from the obvious hygienic benefits, plus massages and personal grooming, it was also an occasion for socializing and relaxing conversations, when board games such as tabula would be enjoyed. For sheer scale and grandeur, the most impressive bathhouses were often to be found at legionary fortresses such as Caerleon (see pages 122–31), where in addition to bathing and cleansing the soldiers exercised in a covered hall and outdoor swimming pool. Most civilian bathhouses were designed just for washing and cleansing, but there were actual purpose-built swimming pools at Bath and Buxton.

centaury (a delicate pink flower of the gentian family) and woodland birds such as blackcap, nuthatch and woodpecker.

At Home With the Romans

Chedworth Roman Villa was founded about AD 120 above the River Coln (which eventually flows into the Thames near Fairford), and is one of nine similar villas in a 5-mile radius. Like the others featured in this book, the villa evolved over successive centuries, with new owners adding rooms and adapting others. It began as three separate but modest groups of buildings, but after much rebuilding ended up a grand mansion. In shape it resembled a three-sided rectangle, with two long wings enclosing a courtyard garden, and eventually the complex included heated dining rooms and bedrooms, plus two bathhouses and kitchens.

The villa was discovered in 1864 and after initial excavations, when the mock-Tudor house in which the small museum is sited was built, Chedworth passed into the hands of

the National Trust. Today's visitors can see a short audio-visual presentation and also some of the ongoing digs, as well as enjoy a range of other events from March to September that include Romano-British craft days, kiln-building and pottery demonstrations, plus activities for children.

Although most of the south wing has not been excavated, the north and west wings have revealed a series of rooms and areas that show what went on in the daily life of a Roman villa. One of the first rooms you will come to is the dining room (*triclinium*), complete with a well-preserved mosaic floor. The pattern is in two halves: the simple but beautiful geometric pattern on the right is where the diners would sit and eat, while the mytho-logical scene laid out in colourful and intricate *tesserae* (tiny cubes of different coloured stone – see the feature on page 103) would have been left open to be viewed and admired. Among other things, the mosaic depicts the four seasons, and although Autumn is damaged you can still see Summer clutching a basket of flowers and Winter holding a dead hare and a leafless branch. The mosaicists almost certainly operated from a workshop in Cirencester and were responsible for designing and laying mosaic floors and pavements in many other local buildings. Some of their work is on show at the Corinium Museum in Cirencester (see below).

A gaping hole in the dining floor reveals the hypocaust or underground central heating system that kept the room warm. Here it is a series of channels, but on the north wing is a different style altogether. Room No 26, a heated living room, reveals well-preserved *pilae* – a series of pre-carved limestone pillars – that underpinned the floor.

Particularly striking at Chedworth are the two separate and entirely different bathhouses. Next to the dining room on the west wing was the damp-heat experience, creating the hot and steamy conditions found in a Turkish bath today. It was heated by an outdoor furnace, and the heat was carried up through the rooms by flues or chimneys made from hollow clay tiles (*tubuli*), which you can still make out in the walls – although they would have been hidden behind plaster in the Romans' day. As usual, there were the various small rooms that you passed through in succession in order to work up a sweat, scrape off the impurities, then cool down (see the feature on page 95). Across the garden courtyard, however, was a second bath-house that offered the dry-heat encounter of what we would today call a sauna. Known as the *laconicum*, there were two semi-circular sweating chambers where you would suffer the stifling dry heat; then, when you had had enough, it was next door for the shock of jumping into the cold plunge pool.

A natural spring emerges in the north-west corner of the villa complex, between and behind the bathhouses,

which were obviously sited to take advantage of this water source. Indeed, the spring was possibly the reason that the villa was established at this particular location in the valley, and it clearly played an important role. Not only did it provide fresh water and flush the sewer of the latrine (which is identifiable, by the way), it was also where a special shrine was built. The *nymphaeum* was a small, open temple, probably with pillars, dedicated to the spirit of the spring, and was typical of such shrines devoted to aspects of nature such as water. However, it has also led some people to question whether Chedworth was a farming estate in the conventional Roman-villa style, or whether it was a religious centre of some sort. Either way, the shrine to the water goddess also contained an octagonal pool that held over 4,000 litres of water; although for such a large villa, an additional reservoir might have been constructed.

Between the two wings is a courtyard that possibly held a small garden, although when excavations here failed to reveal anything significant it was suggested that perhaps this was simply an open space. The National Trust have a seasonal barrow of so-called 'Roman plants' for sale at Chedworth, and it's interesting to note how many plants and herbs common to our gardens and kitchens came over with the Romans. Presently to the east of the courtyard is the small on-site museum, situated in the Custodian's House. It includes a range of finds from not just Chedworth but further afield, including remains of Roman temples and a portable altar, as well as personal effects such as brooches and hairpins. There are various agricultural implements and cooking utensils, as well as coins from different centuries. A scale model of the villa as it probably looked in its heyday also helps to recreate the scene.

ABOVE: A living room at Chedworth was supported on these small pillars which allowed heated air to circulate beneath the room's floor.

OPPOSITE, ABOVE: Ongoing excavations hope to reveal more of Chedworth's past.

OPPOSITE, BELOW: The hollow flue tiles in the heated dining room were connected to the underfloor hypocaust.

RIGHT: The Nymphaeum was an open temple dedicated to the spirit of the spring that gave Chedworth its water supply.

The Edible Roman Snail

If you look carefully among the hostas near the entrance to the villa from the modern visitor centre, you may see some rather large snails. It's likely that these are not your average British garden snail, but an edible Roman variety that was once cultivated for the table. *Helix pomatia* was introduced by the Romans and is Europe's largest terrestrial snail. The snails were first brought over to Britain by Julius Caesar's army, but unlike the Romans, they stayed on. Although quite rare (and a protected species these days), they can still be found on chalk and lime-rich soils in central and southern England, and since they generally don't move away from their established patch it is said that their presence often denotes previous Roman occupation. Roman snails are pale brown with coloured bands; although they are lighter in colour than the common garden snail, the main difference is size. The Roman types are up to 4 inches (11cm) long and with a shell as much as 2 inches (5.5cm) in height.

From what we understand, Roman cooks used to keep these snails in darkened rooms within bowls lined with herbs. They were fed on milk, to make them fat, and salt to keep them thirsty. After guzzling on sufficient milk they became so bloated that they were unable to slide back into their shells, at which point the cook would pop them into a pot with some garlic and cook them.

BELOW: Many of the villa's finds are to be found in the on-site museum.

Corinium and the Fosse Way

Chedworth's regional centre was Cirencester or *Corinium*, the second largest town in Roman Britain, and although there is not much in the way of Roman remains left standing today, it does boast one of the best Roman museums in the country. Corinium Museum on Park Street has a wealth of Roman treasures displayed in a spacious and modern setting, and in a way that is approachable and unstuffy. There are several fabulous mosaics, tombstones from Roman soldiers, reconstructions from a barracks and Roman shop, and hundreds of Romans finds large and small. It's certainly worth going on to the museum after you've visited Chedworth, especially to learn how the villa fitted into the wider picture of Roman Britain; although there is so much to see that a weekend might be needed.

To reach Cirencester from Chedworth you will almost certainly travel along the Fosse Way or A429. This well-known Roman road linked Exeter to Lincoln, and you can trace much of its passage through the Cotswolds by the arrow-like direction it takes – so different to the twists and turns of the rest of the modern road network.

BELOW: One of the most striking mosaics at Chedworth depicts the four seasons, which was a popular theme for Roman mosaicists.

BIGNOR

A ROMAN FARMING ESTATE

The Roman villa at Bignor sits among the open fields at the foot of the South Downs in West Sussex, 5 miles (8km) south of Petworth, and but for a sharp-eyed ploughman in 1811 the extensive complex may have remained undiscovered. What has been revealed by careful excavation is a grand villa located just off the Romans' Stane Street, the centrepiece of which is a series of mosaic floors depicting a range of designs and classical stories, including the longest Roman mosaic on display in Britain. The intricate and colourful mosaics are especially well preserved, and as you trace the size and layout of the buildings — with their underfloor heating and hot running water — it's an ever more impressive and fascinating place. Add to this the lovely Sussex countryside, and you can't help thinking that this was a well-off Roman family with uncommonly good taste.

Bignor and Sutton are two charming Sussex villages located below the north-facing slope of the downs, and although the walk is described as beginning from the car park at the top of the hill, you could always opt to start your walk from one of the two main villages — especially as Sutton has a particularly handsome pub that serves good food. The Roman villa itself is still owned and run by the Tupper family, descendants of George Tupper, whose plough hit something hard and rather curious almost two centuries ago. It was probably the water basin or *piscina*, now on display at the villa, and as further discoveries were made Bignor's fame began to grow. Samuel Lysons, a leading antiquary of the day, supervised the early excavations, and soon covered buildings were erected over the mosaics to protect them from the weather and overeager souvenir hunters. The small thatched buildings dotted about the fields look at first sight a little incongruous, but the treasures they hold are well worth an unhurried inspection.

The villa is open to visitors from the beginning of March to the end of October (but closed on Mondays); between May and October it opens daily. There is a small museum, shop and café, plus a grassy area outside on which you can bask in the sunshine and enjoy the terrific views of the South Downs.

To begin the walk, leave the National Trust's open hilltop car park in an easterly direction, following the South Downs Way along a broad and unsurfaced track across the fields.

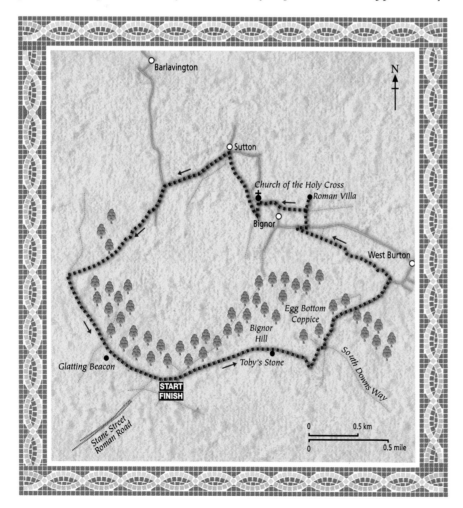

Passing the rounded summit of Bignor Hill, there are lovely views across the downs towards the Arun valley, with Littlehampton and the coast away to the south. A low stepped memorial known as the 'Toby Stone' commemorates James Wentworth Fitzwilliam Toby (1885–1955), a local huntsman and Master of the Foxhounds Association.

The South Downs Way was the first National Trail to be opened for walkers, cyclists and horse-riders, and extends 101 miles (161km) across the downs from Eastbourne to Winchester. Highlights include the giant chalk cliffs of Beachy Head and the Seven Sisters, panoramic viewpoints like Ditchling Beacon, and landmarks such as Chanctonbury Ring

ABOVE: The thatched huts at Bignor may seem old in themselves, but their contents are of a far greater antiquity.

BIGNOR, WEST SUSSEX

Start & finish: National Trust car park on Bignor Hill, GR 975129
Distance: 6½ miles/11km
Time: 4–5 hours
Terrain: Rough downland tracks and field paths, with the likelihood of some slippery slopes in wet weather
Map: OS Explorer 121: Arundel & Pulborough
Guidebooks: *Bignor Roman Villa* – official guidebook; *Romano-British Mosaics* by Peter Johnson (Shire Publishing)
Public transport: Compass Travel bus route 99 connects Bignor with Petworth and Chichester (Mon–Sat); go to www.westsussex.gov.uk/passengertransport
Information: Bignor Roman Villa 01798 869259; Arundel Tourist Information Centre 01903 882268; www.sussexpast.co.uk

ABOVE: A missing corner of the mosaic in the dining room reveals the hypocaust beneath.

BELOW: The scale model of Bignor Villa shows the extent of the 5-acre site and its numerous buildings in Roman times.

and Devil's Dyke. It's a glorious if sometimes undulating route, but where it soars over the springy chalk turf with far-off views across southern England, it really is a very fine walk.

From the Toby Stone the popular route winds its way down to some old, corrugated-iron barns and a rather confusing junction of tracks. Make sure to take the signposted public bridleway northwards *downhill* into woodland (so that the barns are momentarily at least on your right), not the east–west cross route. This scenic track, which can be slippery in wet weather, drops down beneath the mixed canopy of the splendidly named Egg Bottom Coppice. Often known as hangers, these steep, tree-covered slopes are renowned in particular for their beautiful beech trees.

Towards the bottom you join a farm track, which you should follow until you reach the outer buildings of West Burton. Most of this sleepy but very attractive little village is away to the right. Its unusual claim to fame is the discovery, in the late 1700s, of several elephant skeletons in a nearby field. Their origin remains a mystery, although I like to consider the ever so remote possibility that they might have been brought over by the Romans. Unless you want to enter the village, turn left by a cottage called Fogdens for a public footpath alongside a stream. Depending on the time of year, wild garlic and bulrushes can both be found along this pleasant section. The path takes to a field edge, then crosses a footbridge before skirting another. The high hedge is now on your left, and aiming for the houses of Bignor directly ahead, follow the path diagonally across the field to the road. At the road turn abruptly right, then almost immediately left along the drive to the villa.

Life at Roman Bignor

The villa at Bignor was probably constructed in the middle of the 3rd century, and began as a simple stone building. It appears to have replaced earlier wooden buildings on or near the site, since these fertile lands of southern England had of course been farmed long before the Romans arrived. Gradually the farmstead was enlarged, with more and more buildings extended round a courtyard established in the 4th century by successive owners, who might or might not have been the same family. The new south wing included a bath suite, and more accommodation was added as six new rooms were built on the north wing. It's possible that the villa was owned by a consortium or family group at one time, with new mosaics and hypocausts added to certain rooms but not others, maybe reflecting the fact that some of the individuals involved were wealthier than others.

However, to appreciate the sheer size of the complex, take a look at the well-made scale model inside the main building. The perimeter wall enclosed an area of nearly 5 acres (2 ha), which included an inner courtyard and accommodation, as well as an outer yard with various farm buildings. The modern structures that protect the excavated finds cover just a small amount of the original site, and it takes a while to work out the layout and the sheer scale of a villa that ultimately had over 50 rooms.

THE ART OF MOSAIC

Mosaics were unknown in Britain before the Romans arrived, and are thought to have originated in Greece. They are created from tiny cubes of different coloured stone, called *tesserae*, arranged in intricate patterns. As durable floor coverings, they are laid on to a bed of fine mortar, which in the Romans' time would usually have been lime-based. For detailed motifs prefabricated sections were often used, and interestingly virtually the same techniques are employed to lift and lay mosaics today as were used 2,000 years ago.

Some of the mosaics at Bignor are still displayed as they were originally found, and not unnaturally they have been affected by subsidence. Most, though, have been carefully lifted and re-laid on a bed of concrete. To do this, a sheet of linen coated with water-soluble glue is spread over the mosaic and marked with a detailed grid pattern of lines displaying the layout of the stones. A long, flat knife-like tool is then used to lift numbered sections before they are set back down.

Many mosaics follow established designs, including geometric patterns and classical scenes as depicted here at Bignor, and reflected the Romans' obsession with order and symmetry. Specialized workshops developed to meet the demand for mosaics, and the craftsmen often used pattern books to create a specific design.

To achieve the different colours they tended to use whatever local materials were available, and glass or ceramics could be used if stone was in short supply. Limestone or chalk provided the colour white, for instance, while yellow and orange came from the various hues of sandstone and reds from terracotta. Black and grey were sourced from shale and over-fired tile, and blue and grey were achieved by using cubes of marble.

ABOVE: The remains of the bathhouse at Bignor; bathing was an important part of everyday villa life.

ABOVE, RIGHT: The mosaics at Bignor include the head of the goddess Venus, whose eyes are said to follow you round the room.

The jewels in Bignor's crown — for today's visitors, at least — are the mosaic floors, carefully preserved in a series of rooms. They were laid out in the mid-4th century, and the first to be uncovered was Gannymede. The shepherd boy was borne off by an eagle to serve as the cupbearer to the god Jupiter on Mount Olympus, and is depicted naked save for his boots, cloak and red cap.

However, one of the most visually impressive of all the mosaics is known as Venus and the Gladiators. It is in a room that was probably used as the dining room during the winter months, since a piece of floor has been removed to reveal a hypocaust that kept the room warm, and there are also a number of flues dotted about the walls. The lavish mosaic depicts the goddess Venus, looking rather wistful it must be said, and whose eyes are said to follow you around the room. The small tiles used in the mosaic have resulted in a particularly intricate and delicate effect. Venus is depicted with a headdress and halo, and is surrounded by long-tailed birds and fern leaves. Below are winged cupids dressed as gladiators, and the four scenes depict types of combat popular in Roman times. Armed with swords, net and trident, the chubby figures sparring with each other show that even in rural Sussex the gladiatorial contest was still part of the Roman culture.

Elsewhere at Bignor, a room bears a mosaic of a dolphin, together with what appears to be the signature of the mosaicist. A small triangle encloses the letters 'TER', which some have supposed stands for the designer Terentius. The mosaic along the north corridor is believed to be the longest surviving example uncovered in Britain, measuring 78 feet (24m). It is a simple but attractive geometric pattern of blue labyrinth and red squares on a white background, and was uncovered only in 1975; the full length of the corridor was originally believed to be over 230 feet (70m).

Another item of interest within the villa is a well-preserved *piscina*, or ornamental water basin, fed by a lead water pipe and located near Gannymede. Outside the main buildings are the remains of the bathhouse, where the surviving patch of mosaic depicts the head of Medusa, complete with snakes – it was said to ward off evil spirits.

ABOVE: Panoramic views across Bignor and the Arun valley from the top of the South Downs.

The Villages of the Downs

To resume the walk, return to the main gate at the entrance to the grassy car park, but instead of retracing your steps to the road, turn right on a public footpath into Bignor village. The route joins a cul-de-sac and emerges on the main road by a timber-framed thatched building called Yeoman's House. Turn right and follow the road as far as the church.

Turn left opposite the parish Church of the Holy Cross and head downhill along the lane for about 200m until you come to a public footpath on the right, through a gate below Charmans (a private house). Follow the signs across a lawn and then through bluebell woods and across footbridges over a stream. The large pond at the end was created for the original Bignor mill. Finally you cross a stile into a field and head straight up a short slope. Go over another stile and continue through a second field with the rooftops of Sutton visible ahead. The path eventually squeezes between houses and emerges on the road opposite the White Horse pub (which offers meals and accommodation).

Sutton, like Bignor, is another peaceful and attractive village. Many of the original Tudor buildings remain, including the Rectory. This was once home to the notable rector Aquilo Cruso, a colourful local character, who on being accused of having Popish tendencies responded by preparing his own defence entirely in Hebrew. The authorities beat a hasty retreat and his case was never heard.

ABOVE: The important Roman thoroughfare known as Stane Street linked London with Chichester and passed close to Bignor.

Facing the pub, turn left on the road signposted Barlavington and Duncton (not the Petworth road), and walk out of the village past Sutton Farm on the left. When the lane leaves the houses behind and bends right at a junction (indicated Barlavington), veer left ('no through road'); soon this develops into an attractive sunken lane. Where it bears left, go straight on/right for a public bridleway that soon begins its climb back up to the top of the downs. Keep to the main, sunken track beneath the beech trees, which steepens for a while, and like your descent earlier can get a little slippery after heavy rain.

At the very top turn left onto an open and bumpy chalk track across the airy top of the scarp slope of the downs. It passes to the left of the transmitter mast on Glatting Beacon, then heads eastwards over the open pasture. There are glorious views across the Weald of Sussex and Surrey, and immediately below you will be able to pick out Sutton and Bignor and appreciate why you might be slightly out of breath. In that case, pause for a moment and listen for the skylarks trilling overhead or watch the kestrels swooping down on their prey. The downs are rich not just in birdlife but mammals and insects as well, and if you keep your eyes peeled there's no knowing what you might see. On a quiet moment on my last visit I inadvertently disturbed a brown hare, which lolloped off across the fields.

One man-made feature you will notice on this final stretch is a dew pond. It's in a field to the left, and an information board explains that these shallow, circular depressions were

created to collect drinking water for livestock, since the thin chalk soils hold little surface water. Finally, at the field end, turn left where the South Downs Way joins the route, in order to return to the car park on Bignor Hill.

Pointing the Way

By the car park on top of the downs, where a number of routes converge, is a solitary wooden signpost, unusual in that two of its destinations are given by their Roman names. You are standing on the Romans' Stane Street, which, as the signpost indicates, ran from *Londinium* (London) south-west to *Noviomagus* (Chichester). It was built in the 1st century AD to provide access to and from the 2nd Legion's new base at Chichester, and was constructed of flint layers in gravel and chalk, with a ditch and bank running alongside.

If you want to explore Stane Street a little further, one of the best-preserved sections runs south-west from the car park across the rolling downs and undisturbed woodland, and there are plenty of public footpaths and bridleways with which to fashion a circular route. The raised bank or causeway – the agger – was between 20 and 50 feet wide (6–15m) and can be seen to particularly good effect on the open downland. In the other direction, Stane Street appears to have descended a spur by Bignor Hill and passed within a few hundred yards of the villa. It was linked by a short drive, and meant that farm produce from the

ABOVE: Fishbourne Roman Palace, near Chichester, boasts a high degree of craftsmanship, including some fine mosaics.

ABOVE: The four wings of Fishbourne Palace were arranged round a formal garden, which has been recreated for today's visitors to the site.

villa could be quickly and easily transported to market. Although the villa's size and opulence was clearly designed to impress, it was nevertheless at the heart of a major farming estate that took advantage of the fertile soils and the good lines of communication provided by Stane Street. It has been reckoned that the wealthy owners of Bignor may have had as much as 2,000 acres (808ha) of arable land, plus considerable pasture, and as such they were a major landowner and local employer.

The Palace of Fishbourne

A second celebrated Roman villa in the south of England, at Fishbourne, is also famous for its superb mosaics, and a visit to the site outside Chichester is highly recommended. The location was originally used for military granaries and storehouses during the early period of the Romans' 1st-century invasion, but these were soon replaced by a villa that before long was transformed into a luxurious and wealthy palace. It incorporated a vast colonnaded courtyard and four separate wings, plus a formal garden, a small park and even a private harbour. The walls of the buildings were richly painted, and some were

ABOVE: The Roman potting shed at Fishbourne, where cultivated plants popular in Roman times (including roses and lilies) are once more grown.

decorated with marble imported from Greece and Italy. The style and finishing was of such high standard that it suggests that designers and craftsmen also came over from the Mediterranean to work on the palace. There appear to be several staterooms, which included a throne room where audiences would be held. This led to speculation that the palace was possibly built to reward a so-called 'client king', such as King Cogidubnus, a local chieftain sympathetic to the Romans. At the very least, the occupier must have been a big player in Roman Britain.

The villa or palace at Fishbourne was discovered only in the 1960s when a workman digging a trench for a new pipe disturbed what turned out to be a mosaic floor. Today's visitor can see the excavated north wing, housed in a purpose-built modern building, which includes a small museum. The original garden has been recreated outside, complete with plants possibly grown in Roman times, plus a supposedly genuine Roman 'potting shed'. As at Bignor, there are some particularly fine mosaics, including the famous Cupid on a dolphin, as well as bath suites and courtyards. For more details go to www.sussexpast.co.uk/fishbourne.

LULLINGSTONE

AT HOME WITH THE ROMANS

Hidden away in a leafy gap of the North Downs south of Eynsford in Kent, Lullingstone is still redolent of the peaceful and pastoral surroundings that must have attracted the early Roman settlers. A sheltered river valley, with decent soils and proximity to the markets of Londinium *and the south-east, this must have been an ideal location on which to build a new villa and establish a small farming estate. But it's not clear whether the early tenants were serious farmers or more interested in worshipping fringe cults, and with a number of distinct phases of ownership the villa's fortunes ebbed and flowed like the River Darent that meanders past its doorway.*

This walk is centred on Lullingstone Country Park in the Darent Valley, a surprisingly green and unspoilt hideaway, considering that the M25 and London's outer south-eastern suburbs are just a few miles away. The park lies between Eynsford and Shoreham and is managed by Kent County Council, who run the excellent visitor centre, complete with café and toilets. The park was formerly a medieval deer park, and is famous for its extraordinary wealth of ancient trees such as oak and hornbeam, some of which are believed to be hundreds of years old. The circular route passes through the delightful village of

Shoreham, and if you are arriving by train or bus you will probably begin the walk at this point. The villa is managed by English Heritage, and apart from December and January is open daily.

Leave the car park at the visitor centre by the main gate and turn right. Go over the first of what will be numerous stiles for a permissive path along the bottom of the field beside the road. On the left is Castle Farm, incorporating the Hop Shop, and a visit to this well-stocked farm shop is highly recommended – perhaps after you have finished the walk. The Hop Shop sells, quite naturally, young hop plants (more on Kent's traditional crop in a moment). The young shoots were once cut and eaten by the Romans, who called them poor man's asparagus, and the Hop Shop suggests frying them lightly in butter and garlic and using them as a garnish with fish. Incidentally, the farm also sells its own home-grown asparagus, a delicious seasonal treat that was originally introduced to Britain by the Romans from the eastern Mediterranean. In addition, Castle Farm grows lavender for pressing to produce oil – see Peddars Way (pages 20–29) for more on yet another everyday herb that was popularized by the Romans.

In the far bottom corner of the field where it curves uphill, go through the gap in the hedge and cross the road for the waymarked Darent Valley Path to Shoreham. On the left is a hop garden (*not* called a hop field, by the way), where in summer the hop bines (the climbing stems) grow up strings suspended from a wire frame. In late August the bines are stripped and the hops dried – formerly in the kilns of traditional white-coned oast houses,

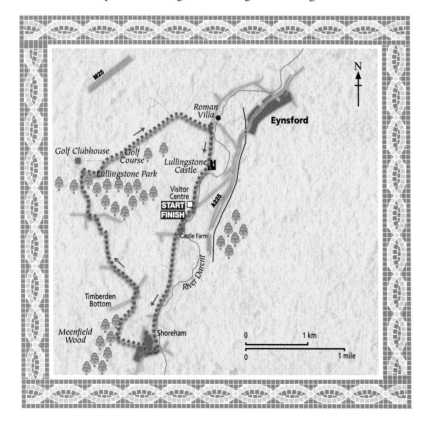

LULLINGSTONE, KENT

Start & finish: Lullingstone Country Park Visitor Centre, near Eynsford, GR 526638
Distance: 6½ miles / 11km
Time: 4 hours
Terrain: Parkland and field paths, some fairly steep, with plenty of stiles
Map: OS Explorer 147: Sevenoaks & Tonbridge
Guidebook: *Lullingstone Roman Villa* (official guidebook by English Heritage)
Public transport: Trains from London and Sevenoaks to Shoreham and Eynsford stations (just off the walk), and the Swanley–Sevenoaks bus route
Information: Lullingstone Country Park Visitor Centre 01322 865995; Lullingstone Roman Villa 01322 863467

ABOVE: The shy River Darent flows northwards past Lullingstone, before joining the River Thames at Dartford Marshes.

once so typical of rural Kent – before being used in the brewing of beer. If you visit the Hop Shop in the spring and are tempted to buy one of those rather weedy-looking young hop plants, bear in mind that it grows up to 18 feet (5.5m) high and will require poles and a lot of twine!

Continue across more fields towards Shoreham, then at the bottom of a surfaced lane turn left then right past Mill House. On the far side of the footbridge over the Darent, go right for the tarmac path into the centre of the village. This delightful place is full of handsome and fascinating old buildings, including Water House (which you pass on your way in), once the home of the 19th-century landscape artist Samuel Palmer. If you turn left on to the main street, you will come to the Church of St Peter and St Paul, complete with its neat avenue of clipped yews and original leather fire buckets once used by Shoreham's 18th-century fire brigade. However, the route goes right, back over the river and along the main street past the King's Arms (one of several pubs in the village serving food daily). This one is especially noteworthy, for it has what is claimed to be the sole surviving ostler's box in the country. An ostler was a man employed by an inn to look after customers' horses, and in this original booth at the front of the building a cheerful, waxwork figure ('the Jolly Ostler') waves at passers-by.

At the road junction at the far end turn right, then in 150m take the public footpath on the left signposted Timberden Bottom. On the corner is the Shoreham Aircraft Museum, stuffed full of relics and mementoes from the Battle of Britain (the former RAF station at Biggin Hill is only 5 miles away), and open every Sunday from May to September. Follow the path beyond the houses up the steep, grassy hillside, then upon entering the young mixed trees of Meenfield Wood, turn right on to a broad track along the hillside.

There are superb views across the valley, and you pass above a giant cross carved into the open chalk slope that commemorates the fallen of the First World War. At the far end, drop down all the way to the road and turn right. Walk along the lane past the first junction (ignore the Shoreham turn) and go left at the second, signposted Well Hill and Chelsfield. This lovely avenue of beech trees (Cockerhurst Road) climbs uphill, until you turn off, right, on a footpath opposite a bungalow. Follow this uphill and past another field and bungalow, then go left on to a lane. After 100m turn right for a path across a field edge and past farm buildings into Lullingstone Park.

Managing the Landscape
The exceptionally high ladder stile (there's an easy gate next to it) is testimony to the fact that Lullingstone was once a deer park managed for hunting, and a high fence once encircled the grounds. The woods would have

provided the Romans with fuel for their ovens and the furnace that heated the villa's bath waters, as well as fungi and other ingredients for cooking. However, in south-east England the Romans tended to farm the landscape for arable crops, and in particular cereals such as wheat and barley. After all, unlike their Iron Age predecessors (and Saxon successors, for that matter), the Romans tended to build stone and not wooden buildings if they intended to settle permanently. The villa at Lullingstone had one of the largest granaries found in a Roman villa in Britain, plus almost certainly barns and shelters for their livestock, which apart from supplying meat and dairy produce would also manure the land. There is also a likelihood that the owners of Lullingstone would have tended orchards and vineyards, given its sheltered and mild position, although there is little evidence to prove this.

Although the Romans were known to have created game parks, it was many centuries after the Romans left Britain that Lullingstone was enclosed as a deer park and the trees began to be pollarded. This entailed cutting the branches at a height just beyond the reach of browsing deer, which encouraged the tree to produce new growth and extended its life by hundreds of years. Hence there are oak, ash and hornbeam trees dotted around the park that are as much as 700 years old, many twisted and gnarled with hollow centres, and some with incredible girths. In addition, look for some beautiful specimens of beech, silver birch, horse and sweet chestnut. To discover more make sure to read a leaflet from the visitor centre entitled *Lullingstone – Trees as Clues*.

From the ladder stile go straight ahead across a junction of paths on a well-walked track downhill. Your passage through the park all the way to the villa will be along the route of the waymarked Country Park Circular Walk, so look out for signposts. At the bottom of the valley cross the golf course fairway (stay alert for golf balls and let the players pass), then go up through more woodland. Out into the open at the top, turn right at the wooden signpost (not left towards the clubhouse) and where the track begins to dip down by a solitary, gnarled old oak and nearby bench, turn left onto a wide path into woods. This

ABOVE: The Darent valley remains an important farming area, although methods are inevitably more intensive today than in Roman times.

OPPOSITE: Lavender (above) and hops (below) clothe the slopes of the Darent valley; both plants were popular with the Romans.

ABOVE: The Roman remains at Lullingstone are housed in one huge modern building.

route continues through the narrow strip of woodland between the fairways, until after almost half a mile it emerges on to open grassland with a fairway away to the right.

Go straight on, along the waymarked route, for a track that beyond a thicket climbs across the open hilltop past the green of hole number 10. On the far side of a line of trees the path veers right, downhill, and with views of Eynsford and its eye-catching railway viaduct across to the left, descend to the Roman villa in the valley bottom – it's just a few yards along the lane to the left.

The Villa in the Downs

The villa at Lullingstone was begun around AD 75 and developed over the next 350 years. There are several different artists' impressions of what it might have looked like during its existence, with an evolving arrangement of living quarters, a bathhouse at the southern end, and a grand reception and dining room with an elaborate mosaic at its centre.

The Roman remains were not properly excavated until the 1950s, and today are housed in a low and rather odd-looking green building that feels, from the outside at least, that it

CHANGING FORTUNES OF A ROMAN VILLA

Lullingstone was one of a number of villas located in north Kent close to Watling Street, the Roman road that ran south-east of London to Rochester and Canterbury, then on to the port of Richborough. Whereas Bignor (see pages 100–109) was predominantly a farming estate, Lullingstone could have been, at least at some stage, the country retreat of a wealthy and well-to-do Roman or Romano-British dignitary. Like at Bignor, successive owners developed the villa, adding new buildings and adapting it

for their own purposes. Originally it was a simple house, with a small number of rooms off a back corridor, but at the end of the 2nd century a bathhouse was added, plus a basement shrine or cult rooms. It appears that the new owners enjoyed some considerable social standing, adorning the villa with sculptured marble busts of their ancestors. The style of these two portrait-busts, in particular, suggests a link with the eastern empire,

and it's tempting to speculate that the owner at this time might have been a senior military figure or administrator. However, some time around AD 200 the occupants left suddenly, leaving behind the marble busts, and for at least the next 50 years the villa remained empty. Perhaps the same Roman official had supported Britain's rebel governor Clodius Albinus in his bid to become emperor, and the estate was confiscated afterwards as punishment? The next phase in the villa's life began towards the end of the 3rd century, when the new owners sealed up the shrine and erected a granary between the house and the river. Because of this, it is tempting to assume they were more committed to the land and ran the small estate as farmers. In the 4th century a Christian chapel was built, indicating that either the family had converted to Christianity or there were yet further occupiers. Lullingstone's end came when a fire swept through the villa around AD 400, and the site was abandoned for good.

might have something obscure to do with the military or sewage treatment. However, once through the doors you realize that the huge, open-plan interior is carefully designed to both protect and show off the entire site, with the deliberately slanting roof accommodating a balcony from where visitors can look down at the whole structure, and appreciate the well-preserved mosaic in particular.

As you tour the covered remains of the villa, peering down at the low walls and foundations below, inevitably your gaze will be attracted by the mosaics that graced the floor of the grand reception and dining room. They are remarkably well preserved and show the sheer skill and ingenuity of the craftsmen. The main scene depicts Bellerophon, a Greek prince, riding the winged horse Pegasus and killing a monster with a lion's head, goat's body and serpent's tail called the Chimaera. Dolphins and mussels surround the scene and indicate Bellerophon's journey across the seas. The four corners show the different seasons of the year, although Summer was sadly destroyed by an 18th-century fencepost.

The Bellerophon mosaic is surrounded by geometric designs and patterns, including the swastika symbol, while on the edge of the floor is a semi-circular apse with its own separate

ABOVE: Lullingstone's impressive mosaics feature mythological scenes, including the rape of Europa by Jupiter, who is disguised as a bull.

design. This small space was probably lined with couches and cushions so that the diners could recline and enjoy the mosaic in front of them, as well as looking out across the building's east veranda and over the valley below. This part of the mosaic is known as the 'Rape of Europa', and shows the princess Europa being abducted by the Roman god Jupiter disguised as a bull, flanked on either side by winged cupids. The diners would also have been able to read the verse couplet reproduced, rather unusually, above the scene. It is a short passage from the *Aeneid* by the poet Virgil, and goes something like: 'If jealous Juno had seen the swimming of the bull, she might have more justly gone to the halls of Aeolus.' Juno was the wife of Jupiter who turns to Aeolus, ruler of wind and storms, to upset Jupiter's nefarious plans. The fact that Lullingstone's owner incorporated lines from Virgil in his mosaics indicates that he was not just wealthy but probably well educated as well (or wanted to appear as such!).

Worship at Lullingstone

One of the first rooms you see on the tour at Lullingstone is the so-called Deep Room, which along with the cult rooms appears to have been used for cult-worship early in the

ABOVE: *Remains of the bathhouse have been unearthed at Lullingstone, with the cold plunge pool distinct at the far end.*

villa's life. In a niche you can see remnants from a painted scene of three water nymphs, suggesting that at some point there was worship of a water cult, perhaps not unnaturally since the River Darent flows just a short distance away. A pit was also sunk in the room to hold the ritual water.

In around AD 360–70, when the cult rooms had been removed, a chapel was developed at the eastern end of the villa, and like the tiny church uncovered at Silchester (see pages 45–46), it is believed to be one of the earliest sites of Christian worship found in northern Europe. On the wall were painted six standing figures with their arms outstretched (as early Christians tended to pray). The human figures are wearing long-sleeved tunics and are adorned with beaded sashes. Although the wall collapsed into a lower room, the original painted plaster was painstakingly put back together and is now on show at the British Museum, with a detailed reproduction at the villa. It's interesting that the subject matter of the mosaics, side by side with the new chapel, has a clear link with an overriding Christian theme. In many ways, Bellerophon's slaying of the Chimaera represents the conquest of good over evil, and like George and the Dragon is laden with powerful symbolic value.

RIGHT: The so-called Deep Room was used for cult worship, and a niche in the wall reveals the remains of an early painting of three water nymphs.

RIGHT: The villa at Lullingstone has yielded many interesting finds, including these well-preserved pots and beakers.

Other exhibits at Lullingstone also demonstrate ritualistic practice. A partly decayed lead coffin, decorated by what appear to be embossed seashells, contains the skeleton of a young man. Another of a woman, also in her 20s, was removed by grave robbers, but bits of bone and coffin were left behind for the archaeologists; both had been housed in a mausoleum in the grounds at the back of the villa. They included items offered up to the gods for the journey to the Underworld, such as flagons and pots of food and drink. Also on display are the skeletons of two geese, found in a clay-lined pit next to the villa with their wings outstretched, one facing north and the other south. Exactly what ceremonial or ritual significance they embody is unclear.

To resume the walk and return to the country park, go back along the quiet lane and on past Lullingstone Castle, a handsome period mansion that once entertained both Henry VIII and Queen Anne. Today it is better known for its extensive walled garden, currently being transformed into a 'World Garden', with thousands of plant species from every corner of the globe, by its celebrated young owner Tom Hart Dyke. Both house and garden are open at weekends from April to October.

Beyond the small car park in front of the imposing castle gatehouse, continue along the popular track that runs alongside the River Darent, in the company of dragonflies and wagtails. The castle's lake is partly visible through the trees on the far bank. In a few minutes you will reach the country park visitor centre.

ROMAN FORTIFICATIONS AND MILITARY BASES

Britain marked the edge of empire for the Romans, and on many occasions they found themselves vigorously defending what could be a fragile and shifting border. Boudicca's revolt excepted, southern England was quickly subjugated, but the Celtic tribes were far less amenable to Roman rule. Hadrian's mighty wall was designed to keep the barbarians of Caledonia at bay, and for a while this was extended further north to the lesser-known Antonine Wall. Meanwhile, permanent-sited legions either end of Wales at Chester and Caerleon attempted to subdue unrest in the west, while elsewhere marching camps, signal stations and well-equipped hillforts, such as Hardknott in the Cumbrian hills, testify to the might and versatility of the Roman military machine.

OPPOSITE: Hadrian's Wall, pictured near Steel Rigg, was the only stone-built frontier in the whole of the Roman Empire; it is a forbidding and unforgiving place in winter.

CAERLEON

LIFE IN THE ROMAN LEGION

Today Caerleon tends to sit in the shadow of Newport, its bigger and brasher neighbour across the Usk, but two millennia ago Caerleon, or Isca, was one of the three permanent legionary fortresses in the province of Britannia. The settlement was a key strategic location used by the Romans for their advance into Wales to subdue the defiant Silures and Ordovices (see page 15). It's clear why the Romans chose Caerleon for their stronghold, since it's an easily defended loop in a tidal river, sheltered by surrounding hills. Complete with barracks, bathhouse and amphitheatre, this site really does evoke the atmosphere of the busy army base, and with a complement of over 5,000 men, not to mention all the civilian support, Caerleon must have been an impressive place.

The route outlined here is partly coincidental with the Caerleon Heritage Trail, a short, waymarked walk around the town centre looking at the town's fascinating past, including its churches, pubs and other historic buildings. Of course, we are concentrating on matters Roman, and there is plenty to see. Indeed, the walk may take you much longer than you think, especially if you venture across the Usk and enjoy the views back over the valley from the opposite hillside. For a longer countryside walk, why not

consider linking the legionary fortress at Caerleon with the Roman fort at the market town of Usk, further up the valley? The fort was the forerunner of Caerleon, but because of repeated flooding the defence was abandoned. Although there's little left of the site, it's still a pleasant walk along the waymarked Usk Valley Walk above the river, and you can even return to Caerleon on the bus.

The problem with the free car park on Broadway, next to the rugby pitches at the start of this walk, is that it is

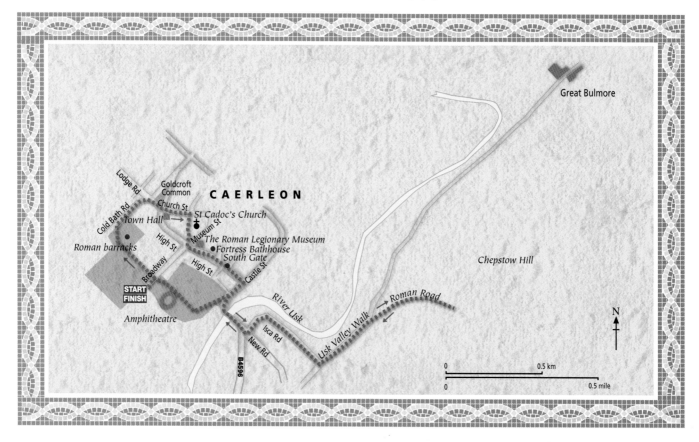

almost impossible to resist running over to the nearby Roman amphitheatre for a sneak preview. However, leave this for the grand finale if you can, and instead follow the sign for the surfaced path (Fosse Lane) opposite, which soon leads to the Roman barracks at Prysg Field.

The four long blocks outlined in the grass are all that survive of the original 60, and are in fact the only visible remains of a Roman legionary barracks anywhere in Europe. Originally constructed in wood before being rebuilt in stone, each cohort had six barrack blocks, facing each other in pairs. They would have been low, narrow buildings, with 12 pairs of rooms housing eight men each. It usually left some rooms free, but in practice they

ABOVE: The Romans chose the site for Caerleon, above a tidal loop in the River Usk, as it was both accessible and defendable.

CAERLEON, GWENT

Start & finish: Amphitheatre car park, Broadway, Caerleon, GR 336904
Distance: 4 miles/6.5km
Time: 3 hours
Terrain: Pavements and field paths, including several stiles and one optional uphill section
Map: OS Explorer 152: Newport & Pontypool
Guidebooks: *Caerleon Roman Fortress* (CADW/Welsh Historic Monuments); *Caerleon Heritage Trail* – booklet guide
Public transport: See the Monmouthshire local transport guide – free from Tourist Information Centre
Information: National Roman Legion Museum 01633 423134; Fortress Baths 01633 422518; Caerleon Tourist Information Centre 01633 422656; www.caerleon.net

were often filled with clerks, craftsmen and administrators. In each pair of rooms, one was used for storing all the kit and the other, slightly larger, for sleeping. The more spacious suite of 10–12 rooms at the end of the block housed the centurion and his junior staff, and included offices where the daily routine of rosters, pay and so on was sorted out.

Nearby you can make out the circular bases of stone ovens, cookhouses and a latrine. This last building, although covered, would have been fairly basic. A row of open wooden seats would have been placed over the drain or sewer, extending around three sides of the room, and next to them would have been the sponges on sticks that served as toilet paper. After use these would have been rinsed in vinegar.

Altogether, the rectangular camp covered at least 50 acres (20ha), and as usual was laid out methodically with great precision. At its heart was the *principia*, the headquarters, with the commanding officer's accommodation (*praetorium*) nearby. The main roadway (*via principalis*) ran through the middle of the fortress, with the *via praetoria* meeting it to form a T-junction. It was flanked by workshops, granaries and the main fortress baths. Most of the barrack blocks were found at the northern and southern ends of the compound (24 at each).

The modern playing fields opposite the barracks were once the parade ground, and you can imagine the footsore soldiers marching up and down and endlessly practising their fighting tactics.

Turn right at the corner of the barracks and go along the pavement of Cold Bath Road. At the end go right, past Goldcroft Common, and across the road to reach the town hall. This peculiar-looking building, built in 1836 as the Reading Room, has now become a community centre, and you will no doubt admire the modern Roman mosaic adorning its front wall. Go straight ahead along Church Street, with the town hall on your right, and then turn right through the black churchyard gates for the path past St Cadoc's Church, which was built (as at St Albans) on the site of the *principia*.

ABOVE & BELOW: The well-preserved legionary barracks at Caerleon was home to around 5,500 soldiers. Above are the latrines, while below is the Corner House.

THE ROMAN LEGIONS

The 2nd Augustan Legion, based at Caerleon, was one of around 30 legions stationed at various outposts and frontiers of the Roman Empire. Legionaries were Roman citizens drawn from the heartlands such as Italy, Gaul and Spain, although this strict selection was relaxed when demand for extra manpower became acute. Each legion was made up of about 5,500 men, including around 120 horsemen, and was divided into ten cohorts, which were in turn sub-divided into six units called centuries. (Just to confuse matters, the exact numbers could vary, with the first cohort often larger than the others. Also, centuries usually consisted of 80 men, not 100 as you might imagine.)

The legions were the regular troops, expertly trained and disciplined, and were moved around the empire to put down uprisings and enforce the emperor's rule. Considerable support was provided by auxiliary units, mostly drawn from the fringes of the empire and often supplying specialist skills such as cavalry, but legionaries and auxiliaries were not allowed to mix. In addition, the army sometimes deployed the crack troops of the Praetorian Guard, a specialist corps attached to the emperor, some of whom came to Britain with Claudius during his invasion of AD 43. Altogether, the Romans needed about 55,000 troops to adequately defend and police Britain during the four centuries or so of their occupation. Legionaries had to give 20 years' service to the empire, and auxiliaries 25, and because of the hard and dangerous nature of their work it's questionable whether many ever returned to their homelands.

Legions tended to take on names that reflected their diverse backgrounds or unique history. The 2nd Augustan Legion of Caerleon was named after Emperor Augustus, who raised it, while the other two permanent legions in Britain had equally distinctive titles. 20th Valeria Victrix was stationed at Chester and was so named because of its victorious role in quelling Boudicca's revolt, while the 9th Legion (IX Hispana), based at York, took its name from the province where it had served with distinction.

The Lot of the Legionary

Ahead is the Roman Legion Museum, and its neoclassical entrance is fitting given the wealth of treasures to be found inside. The focus is, quite naturally, on the 2nd Augustan Legion. We know they served in Spain, then on the Rhine frontier at Strasbourg before joining three other legions for an invasion of Britain in AD 55. Initially stationed at Exeter, they were moved to Caerleon, where their permanent base was finally established. For more than two centuries Caerleon was home to around 5,500 Roman soldiers, and at the museum you can learn more about specific individuals, resplendent as life-size models in full uniform and weaponry. Rufinius Primus, for instance, was a centurion from the 1st century, and unlike the more junior Gaius Valerius Victor, a standard-bearer and legionary, he wore his sword on his left and dagger on his right, plus a mail-shirt rather than plate armour. As a centurion, he would have risen through the ranks and been a tough and uncompromising disciplinarian.

ABOVE: Stand to attention! A legionary and a standard bearer on guard at the excellent National Roman Legion Museum at Caerleon.

As if to demonstrate this, we also learn that Rufinius carried a sturdy vine stick as both a symbol of authority and 'for use in corporal punishment'. The unfortunate recipient of the vine stick might well have been Valerius Martialis, a rank and file soldier whose day-to-day life as a lowly 'squaddie' would likely have been grim and unenviable.

In addition to their weaponry, Roman soldiers were expected to carry all their own equipment (including cooking gear) when they marched along even the most demanding upland roads like Sarn Helen (see pages 12–19). Although highly trained combatants, legionaries were also required to carry out much of the building and construction work associated with the Romans' military expansion. Thus we find that Hadrian's Wall was built not by auxiliaries or hired labour but mostly by the legionaries themselves. They were also required to quarry stone and lay roads, so that the troops were not just a trained fighting force but also expert surveyors and engineers. Many of the outstanding Roman constructions still evident in Britain today, such as Hadrian's Wall and the amphitheatre here at Caerleon, bear inscriptions by the very soldiers whose backbreaking efforts created them.

The Roman Legion Museum is free to enter, and during the year there tend to be all manner of special events held around the town celebrating Roman themes. Talks and workshops (everything from Roman food to medicine) go hand in hand, as it were, with costume re-enactments in the amphitheatre. During the school holidays a full-size Roman barrack room is recreated, and you can try on replica armour.

Walk along the High Street from the museum past the tourist information centre to the fortress bathhouse (there's an admission charge). The remains of this important establishment, now covered, include an outdoor pool with an elaborate shrine at its head, an aisled exercise hall and changing rooms heated by a hypocaust – not to mention the warm, hot and cold baths. Altogether it was a vast complex, and with a high vaulted roof rather like a grand religious building. In addition to its hygienic and health-giving properties, it also served an important social role and helped take the troops away from the toils of everyday military duty. Described as a cross between a modern leisure centre and a gentlemen's club, the baths included galleries and a library, and refreshments were also served. Sporting games took place in the exercise hall or outside in the open air, and the swimming pool, 135 feet (41m) long and shelving from one end to the other, was fed by a continuous flow of water. The outline of the pool, shortened in subsequent years, is revealed in the museum. But the bathhouse was also a key place for discussions and private conversations, and a place for the troops to unwind. Outside the fortress, among the civilian buildings, there were almost certainly smaller bathhouses, but the grandest was of course reserved for the troops. For more on Roman bathing, see Chedworth (pages 90–99).

Carry on along the road past the pubs and shops until you come to a plaque in the pavement marking the original location of the South Gate, one of four in the 52-acre (21-ha) military fortress. Cross the road to look around the arts and crafts centre opposite, which incorporates a goldsmith's, a gallery and a sculpture garden. Already you will have noticed a

ABOVE: The Roman baths at Caerleon were a cross between a leisure centre and a gentleman's club.

series of huge wooden sculptures dotted all over the town, including one of a Roman soldier and Celtic woman outside the Roman Legion Museum. There are a dozen in all, crafted by sculptors from as far afield as Bulgaria and the Czech Republic, and a local leaflet describes a short trail that visits them all.

At the end of the High Street swing right past the Hanbury Arms, with its enticing terrace above the river, and crossing the road go over the bridge above the tidal Usk. The Romans constructed a wooden bridge a little upstream from the pub, but the present version replaced an equally historic wooden crossing that had stood since the Middle Ages. However, most of it was washed away by a flood one night in 1772, and unfortunately it took with it a Mrs Williams, who was crossing the bridge at the time. According to the tale, Mrs Williams was out looking for her husband, whom she suspected was propping up the bar in one of the town's pubs. Heading downstream on a piece of wood at an alarming rate of knots, the combination of her desperate cries and the light from her lantern attracted the attention of bystanders, and she was pulled to safety before she could disappear into the Bristol Channel.

Turn left by the Ship Inn, past the octagonal toll house, and left again into Lulworth Road by the pub. This turns right and becomes Isca Road, most appropriately given our walk, then continues alongside the river to the Bell Inn, a former 17th-century coaching inn built on the site of a Roman burial ground. Turn left and after 200m go right through a wooden kissing gate for a public footpath waymarked the Usk Valley Walk. This is the route of a former Roman road, which winds its way up the hillside among the bracken and brambles, and finally emerges on the edge of a golf course. There are lovely views back over Caerleon and the Usk valley, and the sharp-eyed will be able to determine the position of the amphitheatre and barracks.

As Caerleon was a legionary fortress, the roads from here were well used. One headed north to Usk and Abergavenny, then on to Brecon (see Sarn Helen, pages 12–19), while another stretched eastwards to the town of Caerwent, approaching Chepstow. The Romans established Caerwent as the home of the Silures, one of the native tribes that had so stubbornly resisted the Romans in south Wales. After destroying their original stronghold at Llanmelin Wood, Julius Frontinus decided to relocate the troublesome natives to this new site conveniently near Caerleon. This appeared to be standard practice by the Romans, granting limited autonomy to towns where local tribes could prove that they were peaceful

BELOW: Caerleon's 12-foot (3.5-m) high Roman walls include holes used to support scaffolding during their original construction.

and well intentioned towards Rome. In this way many pre-Roman tribes were recognized in the Romans' *civitates*, or administrative regions, and civitas capitals such as Silchester (pages 40–49), Cirencester and Exeter grew to become important towns. Often, as at Caerwent, the new town was located quite close to an existing fort or previous seat of power. The Silures at Caerwent undoubtedly knew that if they stepped out of line a certain 2nd Augustan Legion would come marching over the hill.

From the top of the hilltop by the golf course, stronger walkers may wish to continue via Chepstow Hill and Catsash Road for the path down to Great Bulmore and then the riverside lane back to Caerleon; otherwise retrace your steps to re-cross the Usk road bridge. Cross the road by the pedestrian crossing again, and once over the nearby stile take the signposted field path across to the former Roman wall. A further short field brings you to the amphitheatre and the finish of the walk.

Praying for Divine Vengeance

Caerleon's amphitheatre was completed around AD 80–90, the same time as the Colosseum in Rome, but unlike its famous contemporary, which could seat about 50,000, the arena in south Wales could hold only about 6,000 spectators (roughly the full complement of the

BELOW: The River Usk provided a handy means of supply and communication for the 2nd Augustan Legion.

garrison at Caerleon). That said, the oval-shaped auditorium remains an impressive construction and one of the most fully excavated of its kind in Britain. It's located just outside the walls of the camp, and for a long time it was known as King Arthur's Round Table. The earth banking was created from the original excavation of the arena, and upon this there would be rows of timber-framed seats. The arena itself had two main entrances, with narrow stairways giving the spectators access to the seating. They would have to present their ticket – a lead token – to gain admittance, with top-ranking officers positioned in a special VIP box. As usual, there would be a combination of gladiatorial contests, animal hunting and executions, although it was likely that military training and displays were also commonplace. It was also where the commanding officer could address his troops and bring visiting dignitaries. For more on what went on in the arena, turn to the Chester walk (pages 68–77).

The amphitheatre at Caerleon is particularly well preserved and includes some interesting side rooms or chambers. The role of the beast pen is self-explanatory, and another probably acted as a waiting room for would-be combatants, since there is a stone bench for competitors. Here you will also find a small recess which may have been a shrine to Nemesis, the goddess of fate and divine vengeance (something similar has been found at the amphitheatre at Chester). A lead plaque found in the arena at Caerleon has a dedication to the goddess scratched into it, asking for a curse to be bestowed upon an unnamed person. Unless you were in the audience, the Roman arena was clearly a desperate place.

LEFT: A niche shrine by the arena; competitors would no doubt pray for good fortune in the ring.

HARDKNOTT FORT

THE ROMANS' HILLTOP FORTRESS

Perched on a remote and rugged hilltop in the southern Lake District, Hardknott Fort embodies the determination and resilience of the Romans. They didn't set out to permanently settle upland Cumbria, nor even to exploit its mineral reserves; rather, the Romans exerted their efficient military grip by a chain of forts linked by well-built roads. Their troops would move speedily from one place to another, enforcing Roman rule and crushing any whiff of rebellion. Hardknott was for hard men, troops used to marching through the hills carrying their weapons and equipment, and bringing the rule of law to even the most far-flung outposts of the Roman Empire.

The route described here is an exhilarating day's hill walk, not technically very difficult nor especially long. However, with the sharp ascent of Harter Fell, in particular, it means that the overall climb is in the order of 2,450 feet (750m). Although there are no precipitous drops, one short section of scree descent does require care, and as with any hill walk you must be reasonably fit and suitably equipped for the conditions you're likely to meet. In particular, wear stout footwear and make sure to carry the relevant map. For a gentler alternative, or if the weather is unfavourable and the cloud is low, there's a very pleasant (and easy) circular ramble around the head of the Esk valley from the car park at the start of this walk (just a few minutes from the fort) via Whahouse Bridge and Brotherilkeld.

The main walk begins at the small parking area at the western (Eskdale) foot of Hardknott Pass, by the cattle grid opposite some attractive oak trees. Take the track signposted 'Dunnerdale 3 miles' south-westwards over Jubilee Bridge, a tiny and exquisite stone construction, then via two gates follow the easy route up across the

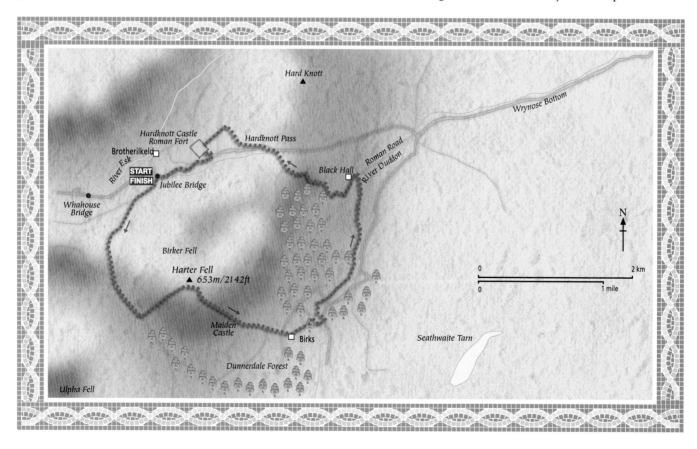

HARDKNOTT FORT, CUMBRIA

Start & finish: Car park at western foot of Hardknott Pass, GR 214012
Distance: 7½ miles/12km
Time: 5–6 hours
Terrain: Hillside paths and tracks, some rough and steep
Map: OS Outdoor Leisure 6: The English Lakes South-western area
Guidebook: *Roman Forts in Britain* by David Breeze (Shire Publishing)
Public transport: The Ravenglass–Eskdale railway is a couple of miles away in the Esk valley (Dalegarth station)
Information: Ambleside Tourist Information Centre 015394 32582

BELOW: The fort at Hardknott was deliberately sited for its strategic views down the Esk valley.

ROUTES ACROSS THE SKY

Hardknott Fort was situated on a Roman route that ran inland from the coast, one of a number of ambitious and interconnecting roads that spanned this upland corner of the empire. Their purpose was to allow swift deployment of troops across the rough and unforgiving territory.

Probably the most famous of these is a route known as High Street, running across the fells to the east of Ullswater and as well used by today's hillwalkers as it was by the Roman troops nearly 2,000 years ago. It connected the fort of *Brocavum* (Brougham), near Penrith, with one located at the northern end of Windermere near Ambleside,

called *Galava*. The route of High Street simply follows a vast, natural ridge that divides Ullswater from Haweswater, and from beginning to end the Roman road extends almost 15 miles and climbs to around 2,700 feet (820m) at its highest point. It is utterly exposed and for much of its distance passes no human habitation at all.

Towards the southern end a stretch is known as Scot's Rake because it was later used by cattle raiders from north of the border, and indeed it seems likely that such an obvious route was probably used by traders and tribesmen long before the Romans.

hillside (ignore a lower path). Already there are glorious views down the Esk valley towards the sea, with a mountain backdrop behind you.

The route continues via a couple more gates then swings southwards around Birker Fell and levels out. Beyond the fence on your right is the wild but rather featureless expanse of Ulpha Fell. When you reach a plantation of young conifers, don't go through the gate but turn abruptly left for a rather steep but straightforward grassy plod up to the top of Harter Fell. As the forestry fence swings off to the right, continue uphill, and although the path is faint in places simply aim for the obvious, rocky summit and you won't go wrong.

Your efforts will be rewarded, however, for the views from the 2142-foot (653-m) top are magnificent. To the south is the low strip of the Cumbrian shore and the Irish Sea sparkling into the distance; east is Coniston Old Man, with the Langdale fells further round, while to the north-west is the mighty Sca Fell range – the highest land in England. It's a terrific spectacle, but once you've soaked up the distant hills make sure to position yourself on the northern side of the summit for a particularly impressive view of your day's destination. Hardknott Fort is laid out far below – it's as if you're seeing it from the air. Look for the distinctive square, walled enclosure by the snaking mountain road, and see how the fort appears plonked almost randomly on the craggy hillside (it's location will make more sense once you stand at the site and appreciate its strategic position). The shapes within the fort itself are the outlines of the former military buildings. Allow your eyes to follow the road over Hardknott Pass to the right and you will arrive at Black Hall, a farm you will be passing in about an hour or so's time, and from it you can see a dead-straight track that is the former Roman road to Ambleside.

Leave the summit in a south-easterly direction, heading straight down the open hillside on a slender path towards the River Duddon. There are glimpses of Seathwaite Tarn on the far hillside across the valley. Go through a gate and into Forestry Commission land – loosely known as Dunnerdale Forest – and after descending a rough and rather steep section of scree past a crag called Maiden Castle, you cross an area recently felled and finally emerge at a junction of routes at the bottom. Go straight across and down to an old farmstead known as the Birks (now a field study centre), and, keeping the buildings on your right, take the grassy path away to the left that becomes a walled track which drops down through trees to a small bridge over the River Duddon. Here the water is squeezed through the rocks in a mini gorge and it is a delightful sight, with tumbling cataracts and deep, clear pools. How tempting they look on a hot summer's day!

Cross the bridge, but without reaching the road turn left for the riverside path upstream. Cross back over via a new bridge at the picnic site, then go immediately right on a public bridleway along the river's west bank all the way to Black Hall.

Along the Duddon Valley

After your lofty travails on Harter Fell this is an easy and scenic section, with plenty of birdlife and great views up and down the unspoilt valley. Approaching Black Hall the route veers away from the river – follow the signs through the fields. Don't go through the gate into the farmyard but turn left (not the seemingly more obvious route right) for a plank bridge and stile, then left again on to a farm track. With the farm now behind you, follow the tractor route across the slope and go through the second gate on your right – look for the yellow waymark that denotes a public footpath. Go over the steep steps in the wall opposite, and after a subsequent gate make your way up the open hillside, keeping the conifer plantation on your left. Glancing behind, you can see the characteristically straight Roman road across the head of the valley from the farm.

At the top of the slope, when the trees eventually cease, there's a good view of Harter Fell away to the left. Now bear right and cross the bumpy hillside to join the narrow road. This is the fearsome Hardknott Pass, a single-track mountain road almost 1,300 feet (395m) high, whose 1-in-3 hairpins send some motorists into a cold sweat. The road is unfenced and the grassy borders allow pedestrians plenty of room, so turning left follow its progress down the hillside for 200m. Veer off to the right before the hairpin for a path across the open, part-bracken-covered slope. Drop down to cross a wide and surprisingly flat grassy area. This was the Roman soldiers' parade ground, deliberately levelled to allow them to march up and down to practise their drills. Because the surrounding terrain is so undulating, the parade ground is particularly noticeable, and is one of the finest examples of its kind in Britain. Beyond is the northern entrance to the fort itself, which is open all year round and free to enter.

ABOVE: Hardknott Fort is situated close to the Sca Fell range – the highest land in England.

The Mountain Stronghold

Hardknott Fort is one of the most spectacularly sited Roman defences to be found in Great Britain. It hugs the rugged, open fell side above upper Eskdale, and with a backdrop of Sca Fell and its mighty mountain neighbours it is an awesome place. The actual fort is quite small (3¼ acres or 1.3ha), but as the drawings on the interpretative panels suggest, the buildings were solidly built and surprisingly large. This was evidently no temporary marching camp. The perimeter wall has been partly reconstructed, and where this huge stone barrier, 5 feet (1.5m) thick and over 8 feet (2.4m) high, clings to the hillside it puts you in mind of Hadrian's Wall. The skill (not to mention the strength) involved in building such a barrier on a rough and sloping hillside must have been considerable, but for a contemporary equivalent you need look no further than the amazing dry-stone walls that criss-cross the fell sides like a spider's web – often at acute angles.

Within the compound the foundations of several buildings can still be made out. There are two granary halls, with rows of low stone piers indicating where the floor was raised to keep the sacks of grain dry. Roman soldiers traditionally ate a large amount of cereal, and in some cases a corn levy was imposed on the local population to provide the vast amounts of wheat, barley and oats the hungry garrisons needed.

The *principia*, the fort's headquarters, includes administrative and storage rooms, including a shrine or chapel where the unit's military standard (not so much a flag but a sort of decorated totem pole) would be symbolically placed. There were almost certainly statues dedicated to the emperor, and possibly to gods associated with the unit. A *tribunal* is located in the north-east corner of the main hall where the commanding officer would have given his orders and presided over ceremonial affairs; his dwelling, a single-storied building called the *praetorium*, can also be made out. The troops would likely have been housed in timber barracks elsewhere in the compound.

The square fort had angle towers or turrets in each corner, but it is thought they were only accessible from the walled walkway. The external entrances were located in the middle of each of the four walls, and all had double passageways except for the northern entrance, which had just a single portal. The gates were originally arched in red sandstone, and there are still some pieces by the main entrance on the southern side. It was brought in from a location near the Cumbrian coast at Gosforth, and inevitably most of the blocks have been spirited away over the years for a variety of purposes. For instance, one of the pivot stones from a gateway at Hardknott ended up as a cheese press at the Woolpack Inn in nearby Eskdale.

Outside the fort's southern entrance you can see the remains of the bathhouse by the approach track. Even 800 feet (245m) up on the chilly Cumbrian hillside, the Romans had to go through their all-important bathing routine, although the thought of entering Hardknott's *frigidarium* for a cold-water plunge is enough to make you

RIGHT: Scenic and spectacular – Hardknott's mountainous location was probably not appreciated by its auxiliary contingent from Dalmatia.

shiver. The small circular hot room, the *laconicum*, is particularly well preserved.

From Dalmatia to Cumbria

So why did the Romans build a fort in this inhospitable and relatively inaccessible place? And who was garrisoned here? Hardknott Fort, like that at Brecon in South Wales (see Sarn Helen, pages 12–19), was part of the Romans' military strategy for controlling the local population and managing any resistance. It also allowed the quick transfer of personnel and supplies around the region. Hardknott was one of three such defences along a 20-mile Roman road that linked the coastal fort at Ravenglass, called *Glannaventa*, through to *Galava* near Ambleside. It was a typically ambitious and no-nonsense route, via Hardknott and Wrynose Passes, and was thought to have been constructed in the mid- to late 1st century under the orders of Julius Agricola, governor of Roman Britain.

Hardknott's location, on a spur of hillside with surrounding drops, clearly allowed good defensive views down the Esk valley, something not at first appreciated when you view the fort from high above on Harter Fell, but it was also only a short hop into the Duddon valley should troops need to be rushed in another direction. The fort was known as *Mediobogdum*, meaning that it was in a bend of a river (the Esk). Hardknott was the base of the 4th Cohort of Dalmatians, drawn from the eastern Adriatic (modern Croatia, Bosnia-Herzegovina and Montenegro). These were not legionaries, the trained foot soldiers at the core of the

ABOVE: *Emperor Trajan, whose military campaigns in Britain may well have resulted in the building of Hardknott Fort.*

Roman army, but auxiliary troops who tended to come from the fringes of the empire and who did not become full Roman citizens until after their 25 years' service, when they received a bronze diploma. Auxiliary units were divided into the likes of cohorts and centuries in much the same fashion as the legions, but they often brought specialist skills such as tracking, or were natural horseman and organized into cavalry contingents (*equitatae*). They also tended to be more lightly armed than the legionaries, and in battle often played a supporting or specialist role as archers or slingers. Because of the growing pressures on the Roman military machine, auxiliaries gradually began to play a more central role, and it's likely that local recruitment in Britain took place relatively early. In AD 211, Emperor Caracalla granted Roman citizenship to the whole empire, so that the distinction between legionaries and auxiliaries disappeared even further, and auxiliary troops became a crucial part of the Roman army.

Because of their place of origin, it's tempting to think that the 4th Cohort from Dalmatia — around 500 men from the coast and hills of south-eastern Europe — would have been familiar with this kind of terrain and the weather conditions, but Hardknott is high and especially exposed to the prevailing westerly weather, and during stormy weather it must have been particularly unpleasant to keep watch from such a position.

It's generally believed that Hardknott Fort was built during the reign of either Emperor Trajan (AD 98–117) or his successor Hadrian (AD 117–138), both of whom conducted military campaigns that extended the northern limits of the empire. Trajan faced growing unrest from the native tribes in northern Britain, ultimately withdrawing Roman troops from Scotland altogether and forming a new frontier along the Tyne–Solway line. But with the Brigantes, in particular, continuing to cause trouble, Hadrian adopted a more defensive policy that sought to strengthen the Romans' existing position — culminating, of course,

in the building of Hadrian's Wall. Hardknott was one of a series of forts and fortlets designed to reinforce this strategy.

English Heritage, who own the site at Hardknott, suggest that the fort was built between AD 120 and 138. It was excavated in the late 19th century, then again in the 1950s and 1960s, when a tiny fragment of stone was uncovered with an inscription that appeared to suggest that the fort was at the very least remodelled under Hadrian's rule. Around the end of the 2nd century, Hardknott Fort appears to have been evacuated altogether, or at least a much-reduced force was left behind, so that the life of this remote mountain stronghold was in fact comparatively brief.

To return to the start of the walk, drop down the track from the fort past the remains of the bathhouse to the road, then follow either the road or the open hillside back down to the car park.

If you fancy exploring more of Roman Cumbria, then head down Eskdale to the site of the fort next to the harbour at Ravenglass. Although the railway line has unfortunately cut through the middle of the site and coastal erosion has probably accounted for some of it as well, Walls Castle (as it's called locally) still has on show the well-preserved Roman bathhouse. Some of the walls are over 12 feet (3.6m) high and there are various rooms, halls and doorways once used by the bathers. Although the rest of the fort has long since vanished, it was once an important shore defence and may have been the southernmost of the coastal forts and watchtowers established at the time of Hadrian's Wall to protect England's north-western seaboard.

Or, if Hardknott has given you a taste for marching out with the Roman soldiers across the Lake District fells, head eastwards for the airy delights of a walk across High Street (see the feature on page 134).

ABOVE: A Roman road linked Hardknott with a coastal fort at Ravenglass, by the mouth of the River Esk.

HADRIAN'S WALL

KEEPING THE BARBARIANS AT BAY

Hadrian's Wall is surely the best-known and most dramatic legacy of the Romans' occupation of Britain. The mighty coast-to-coast barrier symbolized the power, determination and vision of the conquering force, who staked out the northern frontier of their empire in the most conclusive way possible. Emperor Hadrian declared it would 'force apart the Romans and the barbarians', but for the legionaries stationed on the bleak north Pennine hilltops it must have been a thankless posting. Today, with the opening of the Hadrian's Wall Path National Trail, you can explore its precise route and marvel at one of Britain's historical wonders and UNESCO-designated World Heritage Site.

The section of the Hadrian's Wall Path described here is probably the most dramatic and well preserved along the whole 84 miles (134km) of the National Trail, but it is also without doubt the most challenging. The wall crests the Whin Sill ridge, an undulating upthrust of dark dolerite rock that strides energetically across northern England, where the terrain is sometimes steep and rough. It's also high and exposed, so make sure you're suitably equipped for the time of year, including robust footwear. If you feel that 10 miles (16km) across hilly terrain is perhaps pushing it a bit, then split the walk over two leisurely days, or shorten the distance by starting at Cawfields or Steel Rigg. You will almost certainly want to explore the Roman fort of Housesteads (*Vercovicium*), and

to have time to pause and soak up the surroundings and enjoy the superb views. A linear walk such as this is made possible by the excellent Hadrian's Wall Bus, a dedicated service that stops at all the major locations along this central part of the trail, including Greenhead and Housesteads. It also stops just a short walk from the likes of Cawfields and Steel Rigg, and is the perfect, car-free way in which to enjoy a walk along Hadrian's Wall. Alternatively, there are numerous circular-walk opportunities along the whole length of the trail, some of which are described in booklets published by the National Trail Office (see information box).

The walk begins half a mile off the Hadrian's Wall Path at Greenhead, where in addition to the well-served

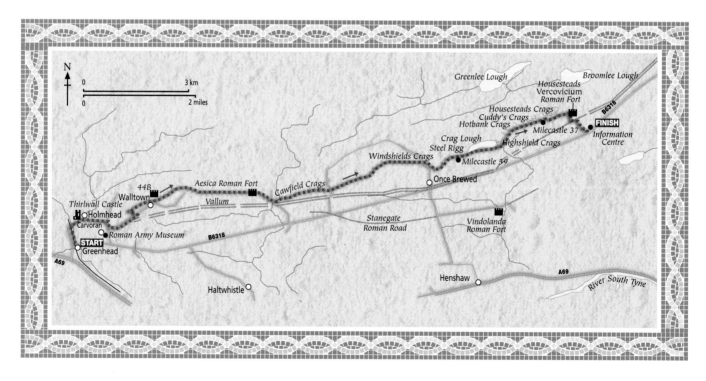

HADRIAN'S WALL, NORTHUMBERLAND

Start: Greenhead, GR 660655
Finish: Housesteads, GR 794684
Distance: 10 miles/16km
Time: 6 hours
Terrain: Undulating, sometimes steep and rocky path, with stiles and steps
Maps: OS Outdoor Leisure 43: Hadrian's Wall; Harveys Route Map: Hadrian's Wall Path
Guidebooks: *Hadrian's Wall Path National Trail Guide* by Anthony Burton (Aurum Press);
Hadrian's Wall Path by Mark Richards (Cicerone Press); *Five Circular Walks Around Hadrian's Wall*
and *The Essential Guide to Hadrian's Wall Path* – from local information centres
Public transport: Hadrian's Wall Bus AD122 runs daily from Easter to the end of
October, stopping at locations along the wall
Information: Northumberland National Park Visitor Centre 01434 344396; Hadrian's
Wall Information Line 01434 322002; www.hadrians-wall.org;
www.nationaltrail.co.uk/hadrianswall

BELOW: Hadrian's Wall looking east from Steel Rigg.

bus stop there are plenty of facilities for walkers: a youth hostel, housed in the village's former Methodist chapel, plus the Olde Forge tearooms and Greenhead Hotel (food served daily from 12 noon till mid-evening). Just along from the hotel, take the sign-posted public footpath by the road bridge over Tipalt Burn, and follow this up the river's left (west) bank in a narrow corridor between the railway and the river. Before long you join the Hadrian's Wall Path National Trail (which has just ventured over the railway), and turn right to follow it across the river by a footbridge towards Thirlwall Castle. In fact, for most of the walk you will be following the acorn waymark for two National Trails: one of the newest (Hadrian's Wall Path, opened 2003), and the oldest (Pennine Way, established 1965), which share the route along the Roman fortification until just before Housesteads.

A Dramatic Defence

It took almost four decades for the Roman army to make serious incursions into the remote north Pennines, following the permanent conquest that was begun in AD 43. From around AD 80, the governor of Roman Britain, Agricola, began to consolidate the Romans' grip on northern England, establishing a network of roads and forts, including Stanegate through the Tyne–Solway gap (which is still identifiable to the south of the wall). For a while this served as the Romans' frontier, but following continued raids and harrying from Celtic tribes to the north, an ambitious linear fortification was proposed by Emperor Hadrian in AD 122. In total, the original wall stretched 80 Roman miles (or 73 miles/117km today) from Bowness-on-Solway in the west to Wallsend, near Newcastle-upon-Tyne, in the east. It was a coast-to-coast boundary that marked the northernmost edge of the Romans' province of Britannia. Although there were some turf-topped sections, most of it consisted of large sandstone blocks, and when finished the defence was

BELOW: The remains of an archway at Milecastle 37, which was built by the 2nd Legion from Caerleon.

EVERY FOOTSTEP COUNTS

As befits such a sensitive archaeological feature, the issue of conservation is all-important when it comes to managing access to Hadrian's Wall. It remains a fragile monument, and a damaged or removed stone can never be replaced. Visitors are encouraged to follow the World Heritage Site's own voluntary country code, called 'Every Footstep Counts'. The main points are: avoid walking on the actual wall itself, which can cause it to collapse; keep to the waymarked paths, which are generally well signposted; and use public transport wherever possible. Those exploring the wall during the winter months, when the ground can be wet and heavy, are encouraged to follow a series of sustainable, circular routes in the general area of the wall, rather than exacerbate erosion on some of the more vulnerable sections of the main trail itself. These circular walks are fascinating in their own right – at any time of year – and take you to nearby Roman sites such as the fort of Vindolanda, as well as Wall Village and Bardon Mill. Locations are promoted via the special Hadrian's Wall Passport (there's even a completion badge and certificate), which can be stamped at set points and encourages visitors to pursue specific routes. Finally, the Hadrian's Wall Path Trust has been established as a forum for everyone who cares about the wall, promoting the recreational and educational value of the National Trail in a way that is archaeologically, environmentally and economically sustainable. Details on this and all of the above are available from the website, information line or local centres.

16 feet (5m) high and up to 10 feet (3m) thick. Altogether, there were 12 forts along the course of the wall, supplemented by milecastles and turrets or lookout posts, as well as a network of roads. Hadrian's masterpiece was not just an exceptional piece of construction, it was unique as the only stone-built frontier in the entire Roman Empire. This was one serious wall.

With all this talk of 2,000-year-old Roman construction, it's easy to overlook Thirlwall Castle, a fortified tower house upstream from Greenhead, and partly built with stones from the Roman wall. Its name is from the Old English for 'gap in the wall', most appropriately, and was built in the 1330s as a family refuge from the cross-border raids that were so common at that time. In recent years it had begun to decay, so much so that in 1999 Northumberland National Park stepped in to stabilize the ruins and preserve what was left.

The Roman Army Museum

From Thirlwall, the trail follows a winding lane past Holmhead and then plods steadily up across pasture to officially enter the National Park. To your right is the unexcavated fort of Carvoran, and next to it the Roman Army Museum, where among other things you can experience a special 'virtual reality' flight above the wall in its film theatre. There's also a café for museum visitors. Mind you, with so many attractions on offer, perhaps this could be pencilled in for tomorrow? Now the trail heads for the higher, open ground, passing the picnic site at the former Walltown quarry, and out past turret 44B and some patchy remnants of wall. Indeed, it's easy to miss the fort of Great Chesters (*Aesica*) completely, since it remains undeveloped, but perhaps this is no bad thing since it encourages you to use your imagination. The most notable feature of Great Chesters was that a 6-mile (10-km) aqueduct had to be built to supply the fort because there was no direct natural water supply.

As you progress eastwards, with ever more impressive views across the wild Northumbrian countryside, don't forget to scan the immediate foreground either side of the wall. To fortify it even further, the Romans dug a ditch immediately to the north of the defence, except where the wall took advantage of the sheer face of the crags. On the protected, southern side lay the militarized zone, comprising in turn a military way or supply road, a broad ditch bordered by two grassy banks called the *vallum*, and finally Stanegate (it meant literally 'stone road').

Beyond Great Chesters the trail drops down to meet a lane at Cawfields quarry, one of several dormant workings along the central part of the wall that have been re-landscaped and turned over for visitors – in this case a car park, picnic site and toilets. From here you embark on probably the most exciting and certainly one of the best-preserved sections of Hadrian's Wall. It's time to pull your socks up and take to the battlements.

As you plod up to the top of Cawfield Crags, you can't help feeling that those Roman soldiers had to be a pretty fit and hardy bunch. You might be carrying a small rucksack, but they were probably weighed down with helmet, body armour, shield and sword; and whereas you will probably be shod in stout walking boots, they may well have been sporting traditional leather sandals or rough boots. If the wind is keen you will certainly feel it at the trig point on Windshields Crags, the small matter of 1,132 feet (345m) above sea level and the highest point on the National Trail. From this lofty position the views, on a clear day, are exceptional. To the south is Cross Fell and the mighty Pennine range; west lies the Solway Firth and south-west Scotland, and northwards you can make out the

rounded shapes of the Cheviot Hills beyond the massed conifer blanket of Kielder Forest. I doubt that the Roman troops patrolling the wall would have been quite so animated about the views, since the cold and damp climate of northern England would have been a far cry from the sun-kissed Mediterranean. However, it is just as likely that auxiliary troops, perhaps some from Britain, were stationed along the wall.

A Remarkable Feat of Engineering

Looking eastwards, ahead of you, the mighty wall rides the switchback crest of the rolling Whin Sill ridge into the far distance. Crag Lough, a narrow and rather bleak strip of water, shelters below the huge dark cliffs of Highshield and Hotbank crags, while high above the wall marches endlessly on in a dramatic scene captured in countless photographs. After you've added it to your collection, too, pause a moment and take a good look at the wall itself. It was actively patrolled by the Romans for about three centuries, after which the troops were recalled south as their empire began to crumble. Over time the wall has also crumbled, although the height and relative inaccessibility of this outstanding section has no doubt assisted its preservation. Elsewhere, in some of the lower stretches, the wall was almost entirely dismantled for building stone, and it wasn't until the 19th century that the efforts of dedicated conservationists like local landowner John Clayton began to halt the destruction. Indeed, he went on to supervise the rebuilding of the wall in some sections,

BELOW: The wild and lonely miles of Hadrian's Wall, near Hotbank Crags.

ABOVE: Hadrian's Wall contains over 70 milecastles, with lookout towers or turrets in between.

including parts before you now. Certainly, the completeness of the wall along this open stretch does allow you to appreciate what a supreme effort it must have been to build such a solid defence over such a difficult landscape. One of the most startling facts surrounding Hadrian's Wall is that the main part of this 84-mile barrier took 15,000 men from three different Roman legions little more than six years to build (it was fully complete within a decade). By comparison, the creation of the modern Hadrian's Wall Path took over twenty. A recent estimate suggested that that a civil contractor would probably charge over £2 billion to undertake the job of building the wall today.

At Steel Rigg car park, a lane to the south leads down to the National Park visitor centre at Once Brewed, barely a mile away, where there is also a pub and a youth hostel. However, ahead of you the wall continues along the top of what are sometimes rough and rocky crags. The actual trail, alongside the wall, is clear throughout and route-finding will not be a problem, but some of the gradients may leave you rather breathless. This is particularly so at Milecastle 39 (known as 'Castle Nick' after the narrow cleft or 'nick' of hillside in which it sits), before the steep ascent to Highshield Crags. Take time, therefore, to stop and admire this well-preserved example of a Roman milecastle, which in its day would have housed up to 20 men whose duty it was to patrol the wall and look out for any potential attackers. Milecastles were built at intervals of 1,620 yards, with two lookout turrets in between. With well over 70 milecastles, not to mention the dozen forts, it's no wonder that when complete and fully operational the wall took over 10,000 troops to service. In addition, the supporting infrastructure must have been considerable, with regular supplies of food and drink, fuel and other equipment being transported here.

A little further on is another narrow break in the ridge. It's known as Sycamore Gap after the prominent tree that grows here, and apart from the presence of the wall, its other

claim to fame is that it was used as the unlikely setting for a scene in the film *Robin Hood – Prince of Thieves* when the legendary hero (played by Kevin Costner) rode up and rescued a young boy from a tree.

ABOVE: A drainage gulley (left) and a hypocaust (right) survive at Housesteads Fort, which is dramatically sited on the actual wall.

Where Nature Now Reigns

The Pennine Way leaves the Hadrian's Wall Path after the ladder stile at Rapishaw Gap, and heads off northwards to pursue its last 50 lonely miles to the Scottish border. Meanwhile, ahead is the final, short dramatic stretch of this walk, beginning with a climb onto Cuddy's Crags for the famous view eastwards towards Housesteads Crags. The wall-builders must have had their work cut out dealing with what are at times very steep slopes, not to mention hauling the stone up to the top of the crags, but there's no doubt that the resistant, dolerite cliffs of the Whin Sill presented a superb natural barrier on which to build, serving to accentuate the power and majesty of the wall itself.

Looking north, the bare and boggy land seems particularly inhospitable, but partly because of this it is an important refuge for moorland and wading birds such as curlew, symbol of Northumberland National Park. Greenlee Lough, the largest body of fresh-water in the county and managed as a nature reserve, is just a mile or so north from the foot of the crags, while the cliffs themselves are home to jackdaws and kestrels.

Milecastle 37 is another well-preserved specimen, and part of an inscription found on the stones here indicates that it was built by the 2nd Legion from Caerleon in south Wales (see pages 122–31). The remains of the archway in the north gate are particularly eye-catching. After this you pass through a small stand of pine woodland, and for the one and only time you are permitted to walk along the top of the wall for a short distance (although there is an alternative route).

All of a sudden you go through a gate and at your feet are the remains of Housesteads (*Vercovicium*) Roman fort. It was built so that the troops could respond immediately to assaults from the north, rather than wait while a force was summoned from the fort of Vindolanda, which was built on Stanegate to the south and pre-dated the wall. Here, in a breathtaking position on the open hillside, you can trace the outline of all the major buildings: the headquarters (*principia*), commanding officer's house (*praetorium*), barracks, granaries and hospital. The latrines, in particular, are the most complete of their kind left in Britain. The 5-acre (2ha) site was enclosed by a protective wall, in which there were four main gates facing different directions. Throughout the 3rd and 4th centuries the fort was occupied by the 1st Cohort of Tungrians (originally from modern-day Belgium), and it's believed that between 800 and 1,000 men were stationed here. There's a small entry charge to the site, but together with the accompanying museum it's well worth the money.

If you want to explore Hadrian's Wall further – and there is so much to see – there are numerous other highlights.

ABOVE: Sycamore Gap – a natural break in the east–west ridge.

OPPOSITE: The Romans' wall utilized the high, dark crags of the Whin Sill, which runs intermittently across northern England.

Vindolanda includes a replica Roman temple and finds from ongoing excavations. There are also displays at Tullie House Museum in Carlisle and the Museum of Antiquities in Newcastle, as well as a Roman cavalry fort on the wall at Chesters and a fascinating reconstruction of a Roman bathhouse at Wallsend (*Segedunum*). Just to the west of Greenhead, at the start of this walk, Birdoswald Fort boasts a well-preserved section of wall, a milecastle and turret, plus an 'interactive' visitor centre that helps recreate what it must have been like to be stationed here almost 2,000 years ago.

To finish the walk leave the trail and take the wide and popular path over to the visitor centre on the main road. (As you cross the vallum, notice the additional grassy ripples, which are old cultivation terraces.) At the modern visitor complex you will find toilets and a café, and this is also where you pick up the Hadrian's Wall bus. As you ride back in comfort, staring across at the distant wall, you may well contemplate that even here, on the northernmost edge of their vast empire, the Romans didn't exactly do things by half.

ANTONINE WALL

THE EDGE OF THE EMPIRE

Although the Antonine Wall is not as well known as its illustrious neighbour south of the border, it was still a strategically important barrier and a symbol of the Romans' constantly changing strategy when it came to drawing its far northern boundary. Hadrian's Wall's pre-eminence today is mostly to do with the fact that there is far more of it left to inspect and admire than is the case with the Antonine Wall, but, despite that, the short (and short-lived) turf wall that once stretched between the Forth and the Clyde is still a fascinating Roman relic, and in some places — such as here at Rough Castle — it is very well preserved. Like Hadrian's legacy, the Antonine Wall was once the last line of defence that stood between Roman civilization and the barbarian hordes, and, since then, this narrow lowland corridor across central Scotland has gone on to become an important location for various forms of cross-country transport and communications — as you will witness at Falkirk's impressive Wheel.

This walk forms a figure of eight, with the main loop taking in the remains of the Roman fort of Rough Castle on the Antonine Wall. The second part of the route visits further remnants of the wall, and could be omitted to form a shorter overall outing, but the terrain and surface underfoot shouldn't give any problems. The walk begins at the Falkirk Wheel, located to the west of the town (follow the road signs). The wheel is basically a state-of-the-art rotating boat lift, built as part of a Millennium initiative to encourage greater use of our inland waterways. The giant revolving structure lifts canal boats 150 feet (45.5m) from the Forth & Clyde Canal to the Union Canal and replaced a series of 11 locks dismantled many years ago. It is an awesome feat of engineering, and although there are priced boat trips, entry to the modernistic visitor centre by the canal basin at the foot of the wheel is completely free — plus there's a café and toilets. Nearby is a pay-and-display car park, plus a park-and-ride, and regular daily buses also serve the site.

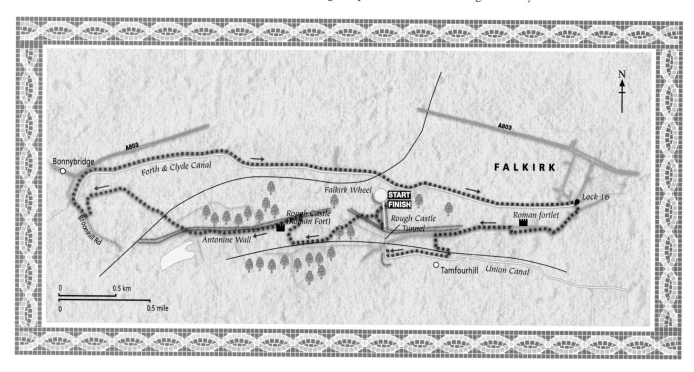

In case you are wondering what the Falkirk Wheel has to do with the Romans, the Antonine Wall and its adjoining fort and camps are situated just a short walk away. Besides, I would like to think that the Roman engineers and architects would have taken a keen interest in the designs of their modern counterparts. The Romans, after all, were famous for creating elaborate aqueducts and sophisticated water supplies for their all-important

ABOVE: The Falkirk Wheel – the world's first rotating boat lift and a remarkable feat of 21st century engineering.

ANTONINE WALL, FALKIRK

Start & finish: Falkirk Wheel, GR 214012
Distance: 7½ miles / 12km
Time: 4 hours
Terrain: Semi-surfaced canal towpath and grassy paths
Map: OS Explorer 349: Falkirk, Cumbernauld & Livingston
Guidebooks: None
Public transport: Bus route 3 provides a daily service to the Falkirk Wheel from Grangemouth via Falkirk
Information: Falkirk Tourist Information Centre 01324 620244; www.thefalkirkwheel.co.uk

ABOVE: The smooth grassy slopes of Rough Castle Roman fort, with the Antonine Wall running along its northern edge.

bathhouses and prestigious buildings. Wooden piping from Roman times has been discovered at Silchester and Colchester, for instance, and the Roman sewers at York and Lincoln are feats of engineering to rival any aqueducts they built above the surface. And, despite their well-known road system, the Romans also set great store by water-borne transport. It provided the means of invading Britain in the first place, as well as the quickest way of supplying the legionary garrisons and many principal Roman towns with much-loved home comforts. The Romans also built short stretches of canals during their occupation, including Car Dyke in East Anglia.

From the entrance to the visitor centre, walk uphill on the surfaced path, signposted 'Antonine Wall', which curves under the supports that take the upper canal to the top of the wheel. Before you reach the mouth of the canal tunnel, turn right for a track across the open slope to a crossroads of routes, and here go straight on (it's signposted 'Roman fort and woodland paths'). Follow an identical signpost at the next junction, and not the tempting route to the right (indicated 'Roman fort') that crosses rough ground and is rather indistinct.

This pleasant hilltop area of scrub and open, patchy woodland is part of a wider scheme to encourage the regeneration of the area's natural heathland, and already there's a variety of wildlife on show. Although you may glimpse a small spoil heap from an open-cast coalmine to the south-west, this part of central Scotland between Glasgow and Edinburgh is mostly green and unspoilt, and provides some excellent low-level walking.

At the far side of the open area the track veers right. Follow this well-used route alongside the railway until the entrance to the underpass, when you should turn right for a path into the undergrowth indicated 'Antonine Wall and Roman fort'. Before long you enter the site of the Roman fort, today known as Rough Castle, and here turn right for an anti-clockwise tour of this intriguing place.

Northern Exposure

The proposal for a linear barrier across the central lowlands of Scotland came from Emperor Antoninus Pius, as part of the Romans' efforts to define and secure their northern frontier (see the feature below). It was built between AD 142 and 143 and ran for approximately 37 miles (59km) from Bo'ness on the Firth of Forth to the mouth of the River Clyde at Old Kilpatrick.

The Antonine Wall forms the northern side of the fort of Rough Castle. Scattered about the site are four interpretation boards which show, in particular, how both the wall and the small, 1-acre (0.4ha) fort was defended. Unlike Hadrian's Wall, the Antonine Wall

THE ROMANS' EVER-CHANGING BORDER

When Hadrian decided to build a formidable stone barrier across England, he no doubt assumed, or hoped, that it would become the Romans' permanent northern border. He had, after all, pulled his troops back from the wilds of Scotland and relinquished the gains achieved in the initial conquest by Governor Agricola in AD 80, when total conquest had seemed the order of the day. But less than 15 years after the completion of Hadrian's Wall, the new emperor, Antoninus Pius, declared that once again the frontier be moved 100 miles further north to a line connecting the Forth and the Clyde, and the Roman troops marched back into a land they had surrendered 60 years earlier. Whether it was simply political machinations at the heart of Rome or a new emperor seeking military prowess, the push into Scotland failed to reap long-lasting dividends. Despite a new wall and series of fortifications that once again edged the Roman Empire

northwards, there were more uprisings from the restless native tribes and further demands on the Roman troops from elsewhere. The result was that the Antonine Wall was abandoned after just two decades, when the Roman high command once again pulled the soldiers back and recommissioned Hadrian's Wall. Despite evidence that the Antonine Wall was temporarily reoccupied for one very short, further period, the wall was deserted around AD 163 and the forts burned so they would be of no use to the enemy factions. But even as the footsore and possibly rather puzzled auxiliaries marched southwards, this was not the end of the Romans' involvement with Scotland. In AD 209/10, Emperor Septimus Severus led one final campaign north of the border, but despite some successes there was no overall domination — if that was what was intended — and when Severus died in York in AD 211, the Romans evacuated Scotland for good.

was built of turf, but similar to its counterpart further south it was supplemented by a broad defensive ditch (see below). There were up to 19 forts on the Antonine Wall, spaced every 2 miles or so. This was much more regular than on Hadrian's Wall, and perhaps reflected the dangerous territory and a greater perceived threat from the enemy. In addition to the main forts, there were subsidiary fortlets in between, and like Hadrian's defence, the Scottish forts were linked by a military service road that ran along the protected southern side. There were also regular signal stations, and since this was very much a front-line defence, there were supply camps at locations near the wall, including a major base at Newstead or *Trimontium* (see page 36), and smaller, outlying forts such as Ardoch, north of Dunblane. Rough Castle was the base of the 6th Cohort of Nervians, an auxiliary unit from northern France and the lower Rhine, and was commanded by a centurion from the 20th Valeria Victrix Legion.

Rough Castle is an enigmatic site: the usual stone foundations and solid outlines you often associate with the remains of a Roman fort are mostly lacking, and instead you are presented with a series of grassy humps and broad lines in the ground, and a plunging ditch that rends the otherwise soft and gentle slope. The information boards help you understand the general layout and pinpoint a few specific features, such as the location of the barracks and granary, but much is inevitably left to the imagination. Indeed, the closely mown lawns and absence of encroaching vegetation, save patchy stands of birch, give the site a unique quality. For me it had the feel of a secret glade or private parkland.

One of the most mysterious features you will come across is an area of tiny pits. In all, there are ten rows of about 20 holes, each originally 3 feet (just under 1m) deep and originally containing sharpened upturned spikes camouflaged with branches and leaves. Devised as a particularly nasty anti-attack measure for anyone approaching the fort and wall, they were known to the Romans as *lilia* because of their resemblance to the lily, with its vertical stem and encircling leaves.

Canal Miles

When you have had your fill of Rough Castle, and its surprisingly peaceful pastoral setting, walk westwards beside the grassy ditch out of the linear site along the quiet approach road. As you will see, there is a small public car park at the fort, but it's

an isolated spot and there have been security problems in the past, so on balance the patrolled car park at the Falkirk Wheel is probably a safer start/finish point.

Now follow the quiet lane down into Bonnybridge. You will see the Antonine Wall marching off across the fields to the left, its ditch now a long, reed-fringed pond enjoyed by mallards and moorhens. The road drops down past a small industrial estate until after a kink at the end it finally emerges on to Broomhill Road. Turn right and walk along the pavement as far as the canal. A diversion along the waterside road opposite will bring you to another surviving stretch of wall at Seabegs Wood; otherwise cross over the canal and turn right on to the towpath. This is the Forth & Clyde Canal, and a waymark indicates 2 miles to the Falkirk Wheel and 6 to Carron Sea Lock.

The Forth & Clyde Canal is 35 miles (56km) long and was designed for sea-going vessels passing from Scotland's east to west coasts. It was opened in 1790, and had taken 22 years to build because funds ran out halfway through construction. The canal closed to commercial traffic in 1963, but like many of Britain's inland waterways it has enjoyed a new lease of life in the last few years, and together with the Union Canal formed the centrepiece of a £78 million Millennium Link project designed to reinvigorate Scotland's two well-known but under-used canals.

Walk along the towpath eastwards towards Falkirk. After the houses of Bonnybridge have receded, the elevated canal enjoys a lovely, rural setting, with far-ranging views north-westwards towards the Campsie Fells and the distant uplands.

When you reach the Falkirk Wheel there is a footbridge across to the main centre, should you need a comfort stop or fancy a revitalizing cuppa; otherwise continue along the towpath for a little under a mile until you reach Lock 16 in suburban Falkirk. Turn right, over the waterway, and then almost immediately right again at the road junction, and with the grand-looking Union Inn over to your right, walk across the wide grassy verge until you reach Tamfourhill Road. Turn right and cross over to the opposite pavement. Within a few paces is a gateway to one of the best surviving sections of the entire Antonine Wall.

ABOVE: The deep ditch and wall are seen to good effect at Seabegs Wood, near Bonnybridge.

OPPOSITE TOP: These Roman anti-attack traps were camouflaged and contained deadly upturned spikes.

OPPOSITE BOTTOM: Easy and scenic walking beside the Forth and Clyde Canal at Bonnybridge.

ABOVE: A modern build ing straddles the line of the Antonine Wall west of Falkirk.

The Turf Defence

Ahead is the location of a fortlet for about 30 soldiers, probably a detachment from the fort at Rough Castle. Along here you can get a real feel for the scale of the wall, for despite not being a conventional stone structure, the depth of the ditch and scale of the surrounding banks are considerable. The Antonine Wall consisted of a solid turf barrier, built on a stone foundation 14 feet (4.2m) wide and up to 10 feet (3m) deep. Culverts were incorporated in the base to aid drainage. On top of this was a timber defence around 5 feet (1.5m) high along which the sentries would patrol. In front of the wall was a huge ditch, which in places was as much as 40 feet (12m) wide and up to 15 feet (4.5m) deep. Spoil from digging the ditch was often thrown up on the northern bank to form a mound called a counterscarp.

The fact that the Antonine Wall was essentially made of turf shouldn't detract from your impression of its sheer scale and strength. The Romans were skilled at constructing such earthworks, and topped with the wooden patrol-walk and fronted by an enormous ditch, it would have presented a considerable barrier to any potential assailant. Here, west of Falkirk, the wall is probably close to its original dimensions, and the pronounced 'V' shape of the ditch is particularly striking. Partly because it was predominantly an earth-work construction, the visible remains of this linear defence are patchy, but the course of the silted-up ditch is often still present under the current surface.

You can walk along this short but fascinating tree-lined stretch of the wall – or, more accurately, the ditch and rampart – for a brief distance. Today it's in the care of Historic Scotland, but previous housing and road developments have made incursions into the ancient fortification, not least a large and rambling Victorian house called Watling Lodge, built where a Roman road passed through the wall en route to the forts at nearby *Camelon* and further north at *Bertha* (near Perth). You have to return to the pavement of the road to circumvent the house, beyond which is a final and much smaller section of surviving wall.

The Antonine Wall now crosses the modern road, and the wide ditch continues amid a long, wooded strip on the far side. There are two points, in particular, where access is

permitted – look for the simple finger posts directing you down there-and-back tracks through the undergrowth.

ABOVE: The line of the Antonine Wall is still evident across today's countryside.

When you reach a mini-roundabout, turn left and walk up Maryfield Place past the houses and flats, continuing on an unmade track that winds its way leftwards and crosses the railway at the top of the slope. Ahead of you is the Union Canal, which was built in 1822 and connects Falkirk with Edinburgh. It's 31.5 miles (51km) long and deliberately follows the 240 feet (73m) contour the whole distance, as well as maintaining virtually the same width and depth – hence it was nicknamed the 'Mathematical River'. If you want to learn more about this fascinating waterway, visit the Canal Centre at nearby Linlithgow.

To finish the walk, turn right and follow the towpath through the 590-foot (180m) Rough Castle Tunnel. The walkway is wide and safe, with railings, but it is a fittingly memorable end to the walk – not least because you are passing *beneath* the Antonine Wall. Emerge into daylight near the top of the Falkirk Wheel, and follow the track down to the visitor centre by the canal basin at the bottom.

Exploring More of the Wall

Rough Castle and the adjoining sections of the Antonine Wall are among the best surviving sections of the Roman defence, but they are by no means the only ones. Callendar Park in Falkirk contains a well-preserved stretch of ditch from the Antonine Wall, around 40 feet (12m) wide and 10 feet (3m) deep. At Croy Hill, about 7.5 miles (12km) to the west of Rough Castle near Kilsyth, the ditch is particularly pronounced, as is the counterscarp piled up in front. The grassy hilltop site also includes outlines of beacon platforms, testimony to its prominent position overlooking the Campsie Fells. A little further westwards are the remains of a Roman fort at Bar Hill, near Twechar, which unusually was located behind and not on the actual wall. In terms of material remains, the best surviving legacy of the Antonine Wall is the bathhouse at the Roman fort at Bearsden, north-west of Glasgow, where the excavated *tepidarium, caldarium* and so on are now overlooked by the bathrooms of modern houses and flats.

INDEX

PICTURE ACKNOWLEDGEMENTS

Pages 24 (top), 71 © Mary Evans Picture Library
Pages 42 (top), 49 © University of Reading
Page 43 © English Heritage Photo Library
Pages 86 (left), 138 © Topfoto
Page 95 © Bridgeman Art Library

AUTHOR ACKNOWLEDGEMENTS

Thank you to everyone who assisted me in the course of the research for this book, especially the knowledgeable and helpful staff from English Heritage and CADW. I'm also grateful to Hadrian's Wall National Trail Officer Dave McGlade for sharing his expertise and experience, Peter Knowles for allowing me to dip into his personal library, the York Roman Festival organizers for their enthusiasm, and the National Trust staff at Chedworth Roman Villa for teaching me things I never knew about edible snails.